coanut Island on Hawaii.

COCOANUT GROVE KALAPANA, HAWAII.

Tourists Scorching Post Cards.

Hawaii
The Big Island

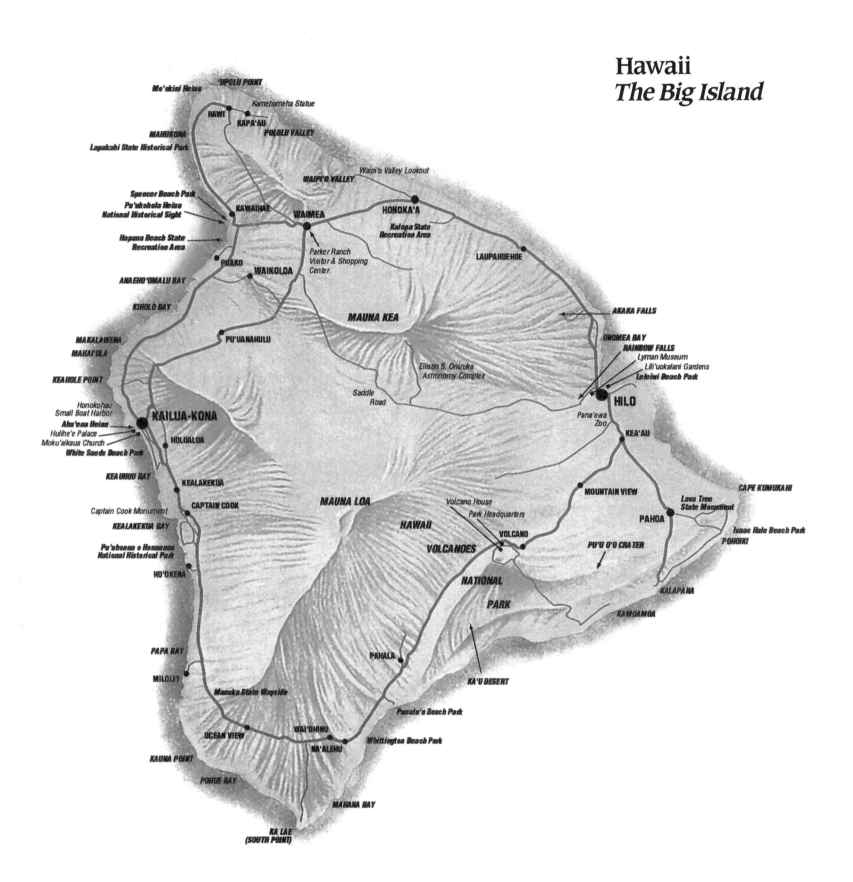

'UPOLU POINT

Mo'okini Heiau

Kamehameha Statue

HAWI
KAPA'AU

POLOLU VALLEY

MAHUKONA

Lapakahi State Historical Park

Waipi'o Valley Lookout

WAIPI'O VALLEY

Spencer Beach Park
Pu'ukohola Heiau
National Historical Sight

HONOKA'A

KAWAIHAE   WAIMEA

Kalopa State
Recreation Area

Hapuna Beach State
Recreation Area

PUAKO

Parker Ranch
Visitor & Shopping
Center

LAUPAHOEHOE

ANAEHO'OMALU BAY

WAIKOLOA

KIHOLO BAY

MAUNA KEA

AKAKA FALLS

MAKALAWENA

PU'UANAHULU

ONOMEA BAY
RAINBOW FALLS

MAHAI'ULA

Lyman Museum
Lili'uokalani Gardens
Leleiwi Beach Park

KEAHOLE POINT

Ellison S. Onizuka
Astronomy Complex

Saddle
Road

Honokohau
Small Boat Harbor

Pana'ewa
Zoo

HILO

Ahu'ena Heiau
Hulihe'e Palace
Moku'aikaua Church

KAILUA-KONA

KEA'AU

White Sands Beach Park

HOLUALOA

KEAUHOU BAY

KEALAKEKUA

MOUNTAIN VIEW

Lava Tree
State Monument

CAPE KUMUKAHI

Captain Cook Monument

CAPTAIN COOK

MAUNA LOA

Volcano House
Park Headquarters

HAWAII

PAHOA

KEALAKEKUA BAY

VOLCANO

Isaac Hale Beach Park
POHOIKI

Pu'uhonua o Honaunau
National Historical Park

VOLCANOES

PU'U O'O CRATER

HO'OKENA

NATIONAL

KALAPANA

PAPA BAY

PARK

KAMOAMOA

MILOLI'I

PAHALA

Manuka State Wayside

KA'U DESERT

KAUNA POINT

Punalu'u Beach Park

OCEAN VIEW   WAI'OHINU

Whittington Beach Park

NA'ALEHU

POHUE BAY

MAHANA BAY

KA LAE
(SOUTH POINT)

HAWAII

The Big Island

A Visit to a Realm of Beauty
History and Fire

CONTRIBUTING PHOTOGRAPHERS:

Nobu Nakayama

Bob Fewell

Lee Allen Thomas

and

Douglas Peebles
Andrew Terker
Hugo deVries
William Waterfall
John E. Bowen
Mark Watanabe
Pat Duefrene
Tom Shea
Charles Jeffery
Francis Haar
Noel Black

Old photographs courtesy of
Baker-Van Dyke Collection
and the
Bishop Museum Visual Collection

HAWAII

The Big Island

A Visit to a Realm of Beauty
History and Fire

Text by Glen Grant

PRINCIPAL PHOTOGRAPHERS:

Peter French

Greg Vaughn

GRAPHIC DESIGN:

Rubin E. Young III

Mutual Publishing
1215 Center Street, Suite 210
Honolulu, Hawaii 96816
Ph: (808) 732-1709 / Fax: (808) 734-4094
email: mutual@lava.net / www.mutualpublishing.com

8 9 0

Printed in Taiwan

Photo credits, Front photographs—End sheets postcards: Baker-Van
Dyke Collection; Akaka Falls—GREG VAUGHN; Breaking waves—
NOBU NAKAYAMA; Lava curtain of fire—GREG VAUGHN; Observatories
at Mauna Kea—PETER FRENCH; Waimea—PETER FRENCH; Wave
washing up on Hapuna Sands—NOBU NAKAYAMA.

Table of Contents

PREFACE

In February of 1988, the State Foundation on Culture and the Arts sponsored a two day conference at Keauhou, Hawaii, the theme of which was "Interpreting the Big Island." Over seventy-five representatives from the visitor industry, island museums and non-profit organizations, state and federal parks and interested residents gathered for a series of discussions and presentations on how the story of Hawaii's largest island could be more effectively shared with visitors and residents. Most participants agreed that while certain districts and historic sites such as Puuhonua o Honaunau, the Place of Refuge or Kilauea Crater, are excellently interpreted for the visitor, the larger themes of cultural and natural history which unify the Big Island experience need richer development and expression. Hawaii still awaits an interpretive center where the fascinating past, natural wonders and contemporary life of her people can be vividly and provocatively told.

Hawaii The Big Island: A Visit to a Realm of Beauty, History and Fire is an attempt by a team of writers, photographers and graphic artists to respond to this challenge by creating a broadly brushed portrait of an island experience. The land, flora and fauna have been integrated with cultural history and contemporary life to tell the story of a myriad of traditions, historic and natural sites and experiences that comprise the Big Island. This work is not the definitive cultural or natural history of Hawaii. It does not pretend to include everything that awaits the Big Island explorer or adventurer. It is an attempt to interpret the whole island through the lens of the camera and the words of a writer so as to provide meaningful insights to both visitors and residents on the Big Island experience.

The theme that has been selected to interpret the Big Island is that of the perceptions of travellers who for the last two hundred years of written history have explored her coasts, bays, valleys, deserts and volcanoes. The reader begins in the center of the island, in the land of volcanoes, and then proceeds to circumnavigate the island in a clockwise direction. The chapters have been organized by district and centers of population based upon interpretive themes that tie these areas into a single ambience. Since there are countless themes in the story of the Big Island, the organization of the districts into chapters is one of many possible approaches. The pictorial storytellers who have assembled this portrait of Hawaii, the Big Island, hope that this will be but the first in a long line of other attempts in a variety of formats to interpret for visitors and residents alike this unique realm of beauty, history and fire.

ACKNOWLEDGEMENTS

The photographs chosen for this book were painstakingly assembled over a three-year period beginning with an initial selection from the stock of Big Island photographers. Additions to this first selection were then made by a review of the files of other photographers who had a special appreciation for the island. Photographs for areas that were not adequately covered were assigned, (which was often difficult to achieve due to the volcanic haze over much of the island caused by the continuing eruption of Kilauea volcano).

In all, over forty thousand slides were examined, as well as one thousand vintage photographs from museums and private collections. Out of the one thousand images that were finally assembled, the criteria of sharpness, brightness, color density, design, and, of course, subject matter determined the inclusion of photographs now presented in *Hawaii The Big Island: A Visit to a Realm of Beauty, History and Fire.*

Peter French and Greg Vaughn with their vast stock and familiarity with the Big Island, were the principal contributors and provided invaluable assistance helping to arrange the table of contents and the sequence of subject matter. Nobu Nakayama's artistic mood images were not available until late in the selection process unfortunately limiting his role. Bob Fewell was constantly shooting local events and people as part of his staff assignment with *West Hawaii Today.* From Honolulu, Douglas Peebles, William Waterfall and Hugh deVries provided invaluable shots from their portfolios, filling in gaps in the subject matter. Almost at the last moment, the work of Lee Allen Thomas came to our attention. Most of Noel Black's assignment shooting had to be omitted due to changes in the table of contents. Other Big Island photographers whose work was reviewed and selected are listed on the full title page.

The vintage photographs came from the Visual Collection of the Bishop Museum where Clarice Maurico and Betty Lou Kam provided valuable assistance. Throughout the project historians Robert and Gladys Van Dyke of Honolulu contributed their valuable expertise and made available their large private collection of memorabilia, photographs and rare books.

Lori Ackerman, Joe Ballantyne and Andrea Hines reviewed the manuscript at various stages for consistency, word usage, and copy editing. Gayln Wong served as an intermediary with the resorts and hotels on the Big Island, enabling their suggestions to be incorporated. Angela Kay Kepler reviewed the parts of the manuscript dealing with flowers. To all these participants a hearty *mahalo* and to our many friends on the Big Island who contributed with favors, ideas, and suggestions, a warm *aloha.*

Introduction: *The Mysterious Lure of Hawaii:* The Big Island

The island of Hawaii often appeared like a mystical, floating land in the sky to the sea adventurers who for nearly two thousand years approached her shores. Shrouded in the soft white billows of clouds, the snow-capped peak of Mauna Kea or White Mountain rose like a stupendous pyramid detached from land or sea. The first sighting of the island from sea was usually at a distance of sixty miles, although Native Hawaiians claimed that even in the darkest evening they could sense the presence of Mauna Kea at eighty miles away. As the noon-day sun

Kamehameha the Great unified the Hawaiian Islands into a single kingdom by 1810. Born in the Kohala district, this great chief left his legendary mark upon the island of Hawaii. □Photo: Bishop Museum

burned the cloud covering away, the impressive view of the three-mile-high volcanic peak looming over the island became even more breathtaking. As one seasoned South Pacific voyager once remarked, the mountains of Hawaii were not as romantic as that of Tahiti, ''but more grand and sublime, filling the mind of the beholder with wonder and delight.''

This ''wonder and delight'' of Hawaii has for centuries attracted the people of the world to explore her coasts and mountains, to marvel at her natural beauty and to settle in her tropical valleys. From the first Polynesian navigators who expanded their civilization to this north Pacific island to the contemporary visitor who revel in her temperate climate, the island of Hawaii is a compelling land that continually invites discovery and adventure. Where else in the world can fire and ice, wetlands and deserts, alpine slopes and jungle valleys all be found within a brief day's journey?

In the oral traditions of the Hawaiian people, the ancient tales concerning gods, heroes and strange foreigners arriving on Hawaii's shores are fascinating and numerous. In more recent recorded history, the list of famous western visitors who discovered the history, culture and beauty of

When Captain James Cook's ships the *Discovery* and the *Resolution* anchored in Kealakekua Bay in January, 1779, Hawaiian civilization was startlingly introduced to Western technology and culture. This 1784 engraving of that historic moment is by William Ellis, surgeon on Cook's last expedition into the Pacific. □Photo: Baker-Van Dyke Collection

One of the earliest depictions of a volcanic eruption was drawn in 1823 as
the Reverend William Ellis expedition circumnavigated the island of Hawaii.
☐Photo: Baker-Van Dyke Collection

the largest Hawaiian island, known appropriately as the Big Island, is
equally impressive. England's greatest navigator, the indefatigable Captain
James Cook, left an indelible mark on the history of the island. It was
Captain Cook, who first charted her harbors and reefs for future western
navigators and described the nature of her Polynesian inhabitants to the
outside world. He made a lasting, important impression upon the young
warrior chief Kamehameha, inadvertently introduced the first devastating
foreign diseases to native people and met an untimely death on Hawaii's
shore. Other prominent American and British explorers and scientists
would follow in the footsteps of Captain Cook including Captain George
Vancouver, botanist Sir David Douglas and American explorer Charles
Wilkes. Their visits to Hawaii would help increase the world's interest in
the flora, fauna and geology to be discovered in the Pacific.

One of the first western visitors to actually observe the fires at the great
volcanic crater of Kilauea was a small group of London and American
missionaries who circled the island on foot and canoe in 1823. Escorted by
what must have been the first Native Hawaiian ''tour guide,'' a remarkable
man by the name of Makoa, Reverend William Ellis, Reverend Asa
Thurston, Reverend Artemus Bishop and Joseph Goodrich visited nearly
every district of Hawaii. They recorded ancient Hawaiian sites and legends,
observed Hawaiian customs, dance and arts, struggled through arid deserts
to view the majesty of Kilauea, climbed to the summit of Mauna Kea and
preached a total of one hundred and thirty-two sermons! The record of that
fascinating journey was published by Reverend Ellis in the *Journal of
William Ellis, A Narrative of a Tour Through Hawaii in 1823.*

Before the end of the nineteenth century, other distinguished visitors
would soon find that a journey to the ''Sandwich Islands'' was not
complete without a circuit tour of Hawaii and a daring adventure to the

edges of Kilauea. Well-beloved American author Samuel L. Clemens, better
known as ''Mark Twain,'' spent several weeks on Hawaii during his visit to
the Hawaiian Islands as a young journalist for the *Sacramento Union.*
Cruising down the Kona coastline, ''roughing it'' to the volcano and then
traversing the Hamakua region to Waipio Valley, Clemens marveled at ''the
loveliest fleet of islands that lies anchored in any ocean.''

Other articulate writers who were lured to the island of Hawaii included
American authors Charles Warren Stoddard *(South-Sea Idylls)* and Jack
London *(Stories of Hawaii)* who later used the backdrop of the Big Island
for several of their short stories. Robert Louis Stevenson's *Travels in Hawaii*
was a series of lively sketches that detailed his 1889 visits to the Kona
coast and Puuhonua o Honaunau or the Place of Refuge.

One of the most astute foreign observers to have visited Hawaii in the
nineteenth century was the widely read adventuress and authoress Isabella
Bird who toured the Big Island in 1873. Her remarkable visit is chronicled
in *Six Months in the Sandwich Islands,* a series of published letters that
extolled the luxuriant island flora and the drama of the volcano, described
the early growth of the sugar plantations and lamented the tragic decline of
the Native Hawaiian race.

As the modern day reader vicariously enjoys the adventures of these
early western visitors an overwhelming desire mounts to join them on that
timeless island, to journey with them through the Big Island's vast
stretches of beaches, lava flows, deserts and verdant valleys so as to
experience another world and way of life. Of course, modern day
technology, science and development have in some places altered the face
of the land. The prominence of the Hawaiian race and civilization in the
ancient days have greatly succumbed to the political and economic
influences of Western society. Yet the alert contemporary explorer to Hawaii

Early foreign visitors to Hawaii often enjoyed the adventure and wonder of a journey to Kilauea Crater as depicted in this engraving published in 1854 in Edward T. Perkins' *Na Motu or Reef-Roving in the South Seas.*
□Photo: Baker-Van Dyke Collection

quickly sees the mysterious lure that has attracted millions of others.

In the midst of the changing present, one senses the Hawaiian way of life that was nurtured on this island where the first Pacific voyagers landed and where the historic footsteps of Kamehameha can yet be traced as he rose from birth, childhood and youth to finally unite a kingdom as perhaps Hawaii's greatest king. The drama of Captain Cook's visit is still felt on the shore of Kealakekua Bay and, at nearby Puuhonua o Honaunau, the spiritual peace of that refuge described by Reverend Ellis in 1823 has remained persistent. At Kona, which was so enjoyed by Mark Twain and Robert Louis Stevenson, the modern day explorer can still experience the village ambience and rich coffee plantations in the upland regions that were rhapsodized by those Victorian visitors. A journey along the ravine-scarred Hamakua Coast is little different today from the way it was in the days of Isabella Bird; and in many ways Waipio Valley is more remote and nature-bound in this age than it was a century ago. And at the edge of Kilauea Crater, the contemporary visitor feels a connection with the countless others who have also been attracted to this place to venerate the power and grandeur of Pele, the volcano goddess.

This pictorial visit to the island of Hawaii is intended to guide the explorer through time and place to experience the physical and cultural beauty that comprise this unique land. The journey begins in the heart of the island, at the fiery source of earth, legend and mystery called the volcanoes. From this vital center, the traveller moves southward and then north through the Ka'u and South Kona regions rich in Hawaiian heritage. In the village of Kailua-Kona, where Hawaiian chiefs, missionaries and history-makers once lived, the pictorial visitor discovers the new excitement and adventure being shaped in modern Hawaii. This blend of the past and present is nowhere more evident than on the Kohala Coast, where contemporary visitors find an indescribable beauty and relaxation in new wondrous resort complexes.

Travelling towards North Kohala and then inland to Waimea, the visitor is beguiled by a sense of ''time travel'' as a panorama appears of ancient

Hawaiian temples, old missionary churches, cattle ranches and the stunning sight of *paniola* or Hawaiian cowboys. On to Waipio Valley and the Hamakua Coast, the pictorial tour embraces images of *taro* farms and sugar plantations recalling a bygone day when a bustling industry and steamwhistling trains cut through the serenity of the land.

No visit to Hawaii would be complete without a stay in Hilo, a Pacific town that has moved into the future while retaining its quiet charm from the first half of the twentieth century. To the south, in a land of luxuriant vegetation and frightening lava flows, the visitor completes the pictorial tour in Puna amid the vibrant colors and aroma of its flowers, orchids and fruit. Hawaii, the youngest and largest of the Hawaiian islands, is seen here coming alive as Pele extends her reach of land into the sea.

This living island is of course more than its myriad physical sites. The Big Island is also characterized by her people. Comprised of almost all the races and nationalities of the world, living in closeness and marked harmony, the island people are as integral to Hawaii as are her beaches, mountains and valleys. Their friendliness greets the visitor and introduces them to the heritage of a indigenous native culture, the influence of foreigners, entrepreneurs, adventurers and immigrants. With their hands, spirits and imagination, the people of the Big Island have shaped a community that complements the abundant surrounding natural beauty.

Through the images of places, people and wonders that unfold in this pictorial tour, visitors and even lifelong residents who are ''house-bound'' should be forewarned that the mysteries of Hawaii have caused more than one latent adventurer to lay aside routine and doldrums for the lure of a Pacific life. An appetite for the Big Island experience will only be sated by the actual discovery and exploration of an island that now, as then, is ''grand and sublime, filling the mind of the beholder with wonder and delight.''

The village of Hilo as depicted in this 1854 engraving in Edward T. Perkins' *Na Motu or Reef-Roving in the South Seas.* , was nestled at the base of Mauna Loa along the peaceful Waiakea River. Although today a modern town, Hilo has been able to retain its unique Pacific flavor. □Photo: Baker-Van Dyke Collection

That Hawaii is an island of fire, is forcefully illustrated here as flowing lava
advanced on the Hawaiian fishing village of Hoopuloa on April 18, 1926 at 5:16
a.m.   □Photo: Baker-Van Dyke Collection

One hour later, the village of Hoopuloa ceased to exist as Pele poured her
lava into the sea.   □Photo: Baker-Van Dyke Collection

These dramatic photographs were taken on April 1, 1946, in Hilo, as a powerful tidal wave slammed into this small Pacific town. Through such vivid examples of nature's power, Big Islanders have learned to respect the tremendous forces of the volcano and the ocean. ☐Photo: Bishop Museum

The Home of Pele: Volcanoes and Lava Flows

Fiery lava pours into the sea while generating immense
clouds of steam. □Photo: Nobu Nakayama

CHAPTER I

The Home of Pele:
Volcanoes and Lava Flows

The volcanoes of Hawaii were sacred lands to the ancient Hawaiian people. In their roaring fountains of fire, the angry power of the gods was forcefully demonstrated. The earth-consuming lava flows that sometimes obliterated villages, *taro* lands and fishponds aroused veneration for the deities who caused stone to melt and the island to shake. Pele, the goddess of the volcano, and her sisters and brothers were said to reside within the dramatic fire pit called Kilauea Crater. Out of respect for her, the island people rarely visited the volcano except for religious purposes and always refrained from eating Pele's favorite food, the sacred *ohelo* berry.

The early foreign visitors to Hawaii showed less reticence to climb to the summits of the magnificent Mauna Loa or Mauna Kea or even descend the steep cliffs of Kilauea to gather hot samples of lava. In fact, the trek to the volcanoes became an absolute ''must'' for the many Westerners who wanted to view one of the world's most active and safely accessible volcanoes. Among them was Isabella Bird who in 1873 rode on horseback to Kilauea, arriving at a small inn built near the edge of the crater called, appropriately, Volcano House.

At the brink of Halemaumau fire pit, she stared with amazement at the lake of molten lava thirty-five feet below. ''I think we all screamed,'' she later wrote, ''I know we all wept, but we were speechless, for a new glory and terror had been added to the earth. It is the most unutterable of wonderful things. The words of common speech are quite useless. It is unimaginable, indescribable, a sight to remember forever, a sight which at once took possession of every faculty of sense and soul, removing one altogether out of the range of ordinary life.''

An earlier visitor, Samuel ''Mark Twain'' Clemens, compared the experience to listening to a Mississippi riverboat with her incessant hissing, puffing and churning. ''The smell of sulfur is strong,'' he added, ''but not unpleasant to a sinner.'' The fiery drama of Hawaii's volcanoes continues to attract visitors from around the world who come to observe the birth of land. Hawaii is the youngest and still active of these volcanic islands.

The Big Island is comprised of five large shield volcanoes: Mauna Kea (13,796 feet), Mauna Loa (13,677 feet), Hualalai (8,271 feet), Kohala Mountain (5,480 feet) and Kilauea (4,093). Mauna Kea and Kohala Mountain are considered inactive volcanoes since they have not erupted for many thousands of years. Hualalai is a ''dormant'' volcano since its last eruption was in 1800 or 1801. Only Mauna Loa and Kilauea remain active volcanoes. Although the long contour of Mauna Loa is far less active than Kilauea, a brief eruption occurred in 1984 and in 1949 the volcano erupted for one hundred and forty-five days threatening the town of Hilo.

The care for the land, flora and fauna that still survive on the slopes and summit of the ''White Mountain'' have become a special ecological concern. At the upper levels it has become imperative not to leave designated trails or to disturb the rock or lichen. In this land of arid wind

and blustering snow, even the smallest disturbance becomes magnified. Hunters, hikers, birdwatchers, sight-seers, and scientists who enjoy the beauty of Mauna Kea have learned to respect the life of the land in a manner befitting the ancient Hawaiians.

Atop Mauna Kea, the island assumes a strange, mystical beauty. Towering thousands of feet above the sea, the crisp wintry air is without the chirping of a bird, the crashing of a wave or the familiar rustling of tropical vegetation. This island summit is indeed a suitable Olympian abode of the gods, arousing a renewed veneration for Pele and the land she commands with care, jealousy and love.

Kilauea, the youngest and smallest of Hawaii's volcanoes, is the most spectacularly active. Called ''the world's only drive-in volcano,'' a well-paved road now encircles the caldera, passing though expansive, barren fields of lava. Trails and points of interest are marked along the way of this famous ''chain of craters'' road in Hawaii Volcanoes National Park. The eruptions of Kilauea, such as the recent Puu O'o fountaining that since 1983 has threatened homes and lands in the Puna district, often is along the rift zone, far from the main road. Visitors and residents by the hundreds view these distant eruptions from airplanes or helicopters. Eruptions in famous Halemaumau Crater located within Kilauea's great caldera may be viewed from the railing-protected edge or the Hawaiian Volcano Observatory at the rim of the crater.

A visit to the legendary home of Pele today should begin at the National Park Visitor Center where movies, exhibits, displays and dioramas bring the natural and geologic history of the volcano to life. At the Hawaiian Volcano Observatory, a new, excellent museum complex vividly tells the story of the volcanoes in the context of ancient Hawaiian mythology. And no visit to Kilauea would be complete without a visit to the historic Volcano House, which is now the home of the Volcano Arts Center featuring the finest examples of contemporary Hawaii's arts and crafts.

The more adventurous explorers can also ascend the lofty peak of Mauna Kea, the world's highest volcano. However, unlike Maui's Haleakala whose summit is reached by a paved road, Mauna Kea is only climbed by foot, horse or beyond the 9,200 foot level in four-wheel drive vehicles. On the ascent, remnants of an ancient stone adze quarry can be found at Keanakakoi Crater and at 13,000 feet one can discover Lake Waiau, the highest lake in the United States.

At the highest alpine heights only fragile lichens can survive. Below the summit are regions of various grasses, low shrubs and a few trees. Mouflon sheep, goats and wild pigs are still found and hunted. The rare *palila*, a Hawaiian honeycreeper bird found nowhere else in the world can still be seen on Mauna Kea as can the Hawaiian goose or *nene,* Hawaii's state bird.

The care for the land, flora and fauna that still survive on the slopes and summit of the ''White Mountain'' have become a special ecological concern. At the upper levels it has become imperative not to leave designated trails or to disturb the rock or lichen. In this land of arid wind and blustering snow, even the smallest disturbance becomes magnified. Hunters, hikers, birdwatchers, sight-seers, and scientists who enjoy the beauty of Mauna Kea have learned to respect the life of the land in a manner befitting the ancient Hawaiians.

The Saddle Road crosses the interior of Hawaii, taking the traveller through the otherworldly landscape between Mauna Kea and Mauna Loa. □Photo: Peter French

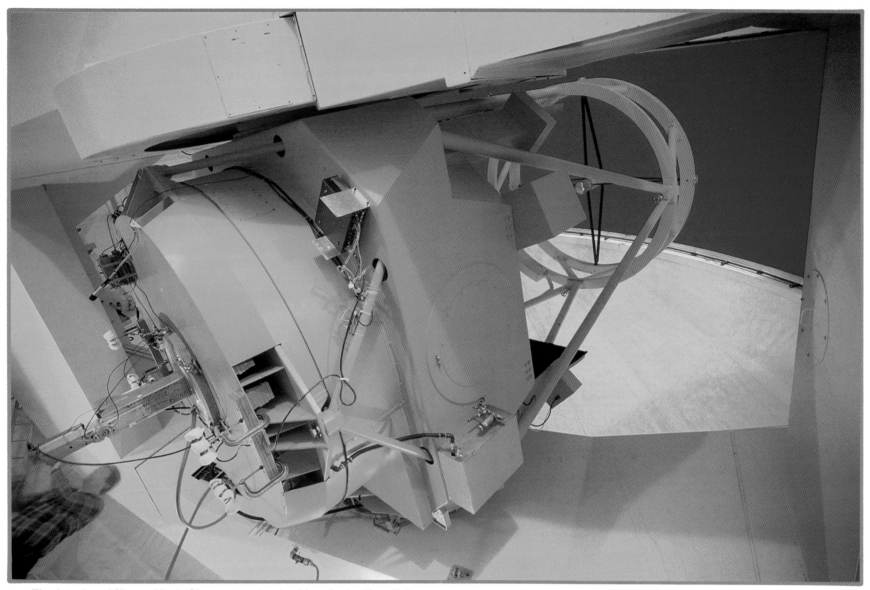

The interior of Mauna Kea's Observatory is a beehive of scientific activity day and night as technicians, engineers and astronomers maintain constant surveillance on the movement of stars and planets.   ☐Photo: Greg Vaughn

Observatories

Ancient Hawaiians had identified over one hundred stars and planets that moved through the Pacific sky and helped them navigate the seas. This tradition of astronomical expertise continues today atop Mauna Kea where one of the world's most sophisticated observatories explores the ocean of space. Located well above forty percent of the earth's atmosphere, the Mauna Kea Observatory site is blessed with an abundance of dark and clear nights and air free from turbulence. Its unique position in a low latitude allows for clear observation of the more southerly stars than can be obtained from the United States mainland or other nation's observatories. Consequently, the Mauna Kea observatory is an important link in the worldwide surveillance of the stars and planets.

The scientists at Mauna Kea utilize a diversity of telescopes including: two 0.6 meter telescopes for planetary observation; a 3.6 meter telescope which is a Canada-France-Hawaii joint effort; a Canada-United Kingdom-Netherlands Millimeter Wave Telescope with an antemma dish of 15 meters; a California Institute of Technology 10.4 meter Submillimeter Telescope; and a 3 meter NASA infra-red telescope. Future space exploration will be conducted at the one hundred million dollar W.M. Keck Observatory to be completed in 1992. Its 10 meter telescope will be able to probe deep space with a power unexcelled in the world. The ancient traditions of understanding the skies to reveal the mysteries of life continues in a grand manner atop Mauna Kea.

The Mauna Kea Observatory is above forty percent of the earth's atmosphere, providing a vividly clear window to the mysteries of the universe.
☐Photo: Greg Vaughn

Sub-freezing temperatures on Mauna Kea frequently drapes the land in snow, thus giving the volcano its name, White Mountain. □Photo: Peter French

Adventurous skiers can take four wheel drive vehicles to the
summit of Mauna Kea to enjoy the thrill of its steep slopes.
☐Photo Greg Vaughn

Mauna Kea and Mauna Loa, Hawaii's largest volcanoes, are tied together by
the lava flows that have covered the basin between these mighty peaks.
□Photo: Peter French

Mauna Loa's "curtain of fire" is a vivid reminder that this
often quiet volcano is still active. □Photo: Greg Vaughn

Maui and Kohala Mountain vividly appear in the distance from the breathtaking vista available from the top of Mauna Kea. □Photo: Peter French

A *hula halau*, hula school, pays tribute to the goddess Pele at Kilauea Crater.
☐Photo: Peter French

Aloha Week *Hola'a*, the Royal Court visits Pele's domain in Hawaii
Volcanoes National Park.   ☐Photo: Greg Vaughn

Pele—Goddess of Fire

Pele lives and is revered in contemporary Hawaii. While many of the ancient gods have been forgotten, the goddess of the volcano still commands respect as her fires and flowing masses of lava often consume the Big Island. When the earth shakes and opens to spew forth the beauty and terror of her molten interior, Big Islanders personify that power in reverence of Pele. Stories abound during an eruption of a strange, beautiful woman with a white dog who was seen visiting homes in an area threatened by the lava flow. Pele sometimes is seen walking in the Kilauea Crater vicinity, and photographers have sometimes inadvertently captured her image in their pictures of the fountaining craters. In her dramatic, volcanic power and persistent lore, Pele will never vanish from the minds and lives of the people of the Big Island.

In ancient Hawaiian lore, Pele, the goddess of the volcano, was said to have lived on Kauai when it was still a young island. From Kauai, this temperamental, beautiful goddess, according to chants, made visits to each of the Hawaiian islands, finally making her home on the island of Hawaii. At Halemaumau, which means ''house of fire,'' Pele was said to live with her many sisters. Her adventures with one of her youngest and most favored sisters, Hiiaka, are widely enjoyed to this very day. The most famous legend involves the time that Pele asked Hiiaka to journey to Kauai to bring back a handsome young man named Lohiau with whom Pele had fallen in love during a dream. Doing as her sister asked, Hiiaka and Lohiau were however detained on Oahu, causing Pele to suspect incorrectly that her sister had been disloyal. In vengeance, Pele covered the lands of Hawaii in angry fire and lava.

There are many current stories told by islanders of having picked up a mysterious woman hitchhiker who sits in the back seat of the car. This ''phantom hitchhiker'' is usually described as being a beautiful Hawaiian woman with long black hair who converses pleasantly on the compelling flames and smoke of the volcanic eruptions. After a short time of talking with the hitchhiker, the driver suddenly realizes that she has disappeared from the moving car. However, a long, single black strand of her hair remains on the back seat. Pele has taken an automobile ride and then vanished into thin air.

Several years ago, during the eruptions in the Puna district that would eventually engulf the small village of Kapoho in fiery, molten lava, a large light tower on the shore stood in the way of the advancing flow. Before the eruptions, it was rumored, a man who regularly inspected the light tower had one evening answered a knock at his door. A lovely young Hawaiian woman was standing there with her small white dog. She politely asked for a glass of water, which the man gave to her. Thanking him, she said that one day she would repay him for his kindness. As the advancing flow of lava reached the light tower, it miraculously stopped within inches of the vulnerable structure. On either side, however, the fiery surf continued, pouring into the ocean. To this day, visitors can visit the frozen, threatening wall of stone that encircles the light tower. It stands as testament to Pele's consideration of human kindness. She had spared the tower that warned passing ships of the dangerous, rocky shore.

Kilauea Crater, the world's most active volcano, is in some places thirteen hundred feet deep and ten miles in circumference. Its impressive, and sometimes fiery vista, has for hundreds of years attracted millions of visitors from around the world. □Photo: Greg Vaughn

Puu O'o vent in the Puna district has been erupting since 1983, covering the lands of Kalapana and Royal Gardens with her rivers of molten lava.
☐Photo: Peter French

Trees once covered by molten lava now appear as haunted, frozen corpses, shrouded by fog in the land of the volcano. ☐Photo: Peter French

Volcano House began in the middle nineteenth century as a thatch roofed house on the rim of Kilauea Crater which provided shelter and food to the hardy souls who ventured to the volcanoe edge. Mark Twain and later, Isabella Bird were some of her more famous patrons who signed the guest book with their remarks on the beauty of the volcano. In 1877, the thatched house was replaced with a small but sturdy wooden building. In this cozy structure was the famous fireplace in which the flame was never allowed to die. Since the nights at Kilauea are cold and misty, the idea of the eternal fire was more practical than romantic.

This first wooden structure was moved several hundred feet away from the crater to make room for a new hotel. Today, the old building is the home of the Volcano Arts Center which sells beautiful handmade crafts by local artisans and sponsors some of Hawaii's most exciting cultural events. The new hotel, owned by a Greek immigrant by the name of George Lycurgus, burned to the ground in 1940. However ''Uncle George'' was able to save the ''eternal flame'' from the fireplace, a feat recorded by George Ripley in

George Lycurgus or ''Uncle George'' was one of the more colorful owners of Volcano House. His tales of old Hawaii and his encounters with Pele became legendary with the thousands of visitors he regaled with his excellent storytelling.
☐Photo: Baker-Van Dyke Collection

The Sun Parlour at the Volcano House was a welcomed source of warmth, comfort and entertainment for the early Victorian visitors who made the trek to Kilauea Crater.
☐Photo: Baker-Van Dyke Collection, 1926

The third Volcano House was a welcome sight to volcano visitors until it burned down in 1940. The present Volcano House was resurrected on this site and opened for business in 1941. ☐Photo: Baker-Van Dyke Collection, 1903

his ''Believe It or Not'' column. A restored Volcano House opened for business in 1941 and eighty-two year old George Lycurgus even tried to harness the steam power of Pele to heat his new hotel!

Owning a hotel at the edge of the legendary home of the goddess Pele taught Uncle George a deep reverence for Hawaiian spirits. He firmly believed in the reality of the goddess, claiming that he first saw her in 1908. It had been ''only for an instant but that was unforgettable,'' he later said. ''Pele has always been my friend,'' he reverently stated. Not only did her beautiful fountaining bring many visitors to Volcano House, but her presence was a continual source of celebration to the awe-struck Greek. Since they shared a common fondness for gin, Uncle George always provided Pele with a bottle, tossing it into the great caldera at each eruption. He also made offerings of Pele's favorite food, *ohelo* berries, in a traditional Hawaiian gesture of respect. On George Lycurgus' one hundredth birthday, Pele honored her old friend by causing mountainous fountains of fiery lava to burst from the earth. An eager Uncle George was assisted to the volcano's edge, where he tossed his tribute of gin and *ohelo* berries to his lifelong friend. It was the last exchange between the goddess

and the Greek who had made Volcano House a lasting legend of the Big Island.

After the collapse of the Hawaiian religious system in 1819, many of the ancient beliefs quietly continued, especially the reverence given to the volcano and Pele. In 1824, the high chiefess, Kapiolani, who had converted to Christianity, journeyed to Kilauea Crater to defy Pele and thus encourage Hawaiians to turn to the new god, Jehovah. While the many accounts vary as to just how Kapiolani defied Pele, they agree that the Christian chiefess challenged the goddess to manifest herself as a true and powerful deity. When Kapiolani was not consumed in flame, her courageous act illustrated her new faith in *Ke Akua Maoli*, the universal God.

Yet, despite this act of religious defiance, contemporary Hawaiians and many other residents still have a respect for their volcano goddess. Gifts of bottles of gin and the sacred *ohelo* berry are still thrown into Kilauea Crater. Volcanic rocks are not disturbed by the reverent, and the stories of mysterious misfortune abound about those who violate the volcano by removing or defacing stones. Pele's lore and beauty remains respected and beloved on the island that she made her home.

1926 FLOW
BEGAN 10 MILES ABOVE ROAD:
EXTENDS 4 MILES BELOW ROAD
TO OCEAN, WHERE IT DESTROYED
HOOPULOA VILLAGE APR 18 1926

With the advent of automobiles, the volcanoes and lava flows became a favored sightseeing pastime for the early twentieth century visitors. Whether it was being photographed next to the 1926 flow from Mauna Loa (above), comparing the Model T being dwarfed by an advancing a'a flow (below), the tremendous steam

venting at Halemaumau in 1924 (above right) or the opening of the road to Kilauea in 1920 (below right),
visitors were invariably overwhelmed by the natural wonders of Hawaii's active volcanoes.
□Photos: Baker-Van Dyke Collection.

The Chain of Craters road winds through ancient lava flows and the evidence of modern eruptions, leading the traveller down the steep mountain slopes to the eastern lands of Kalapana and Puna.   ☐Photo: Peter French

Gordon Fraser roasts a marshmallow in the advancing flows generated by Puu O'o vent. An earlier tradition was to singe the edge of a postcard in the lava and then send the card to friends on the mainland.   ☐Photo: Greg Vaughn

Speeding is no problem when the lava covers the highways as it did recently in the Royal Gardens subdivision near Kalapana.
☐Photo: Peter French

Puu O'o's "curtain of fire" has been providing islanders with a dramatic show of fireworks and rivers of lava since 1983.   □Photo: Greg Vaughn

The Thurston Lava Tube is a cool, subterranean tunnel in the midst of jungle ferns that provides the explorer with a dramatic picture of the geologic forces that have shaped the contour of the Big Island.
☐ Photo: Greg Vaughn

Pele bathing at the coast of Puna creates a wondrous scene as molten lava and the cool Pacific Ocean meet in a cloud of white, hissing steam. □Photo: Nobu Nakayama

As cinder cone fountains and lava flows continue to mark this island of fire, the power and prestige of Pele persists unabated. ☐Photo: Lee Allen Thomas

Southward into History: Ka'u and Kealakekua

Historic Kealakekua Bay has changed but little from the day when Captain James Cook sailed into her tranquil waters. ☐ Photo: Greg Vaughn

CHAPTER II

Southward into History: Ka'u and Kealakekua

Ka Lae or South Point with its lonely, black lava rock shore and windswept lands, seems empty and haunted now. The stone foundation of a *heiau* or temple and the evidence of ancient house sites and village life can still be found along this historic coast. They bear witness to a Polynesian civilization which was first established at this important shore over sixteen hundred years ago and then extended throughout the Hawaiian archipelago, evolving into a complex culture now remembered as the Hawaiian *na kahiko*, the old ways.

It was a way of life intricately bound to the gods, nature and human needs and aspirations. The rhythms of life were maintained through a variety of *kapu* or laws that emanated from the gods and were maintained by the *alii*, chiefs and *kahuna*, priests. From personal hygiene, to relations between the sexes, the care of children, the patterns of planting, harvest, hunting and fishing, all of life in the *na kahiko* was ordered with respect for the gods that pervaded the earth, sea, air and fire. From the simplest activity of planting a *taro* bulb to the complex ceremonies in the temples, life in ancient Hawaii was an invocation of divine blessing and guidance.

The division of an island into several *ahupuaa* or land sections typified the simple spiritual harmony that Hawaiians sought to maintain. Those who lived upland or *mauka* in the *ahupuaa* terraced the land and planted *taro*, sweet potatoes and other food stuffs which was bartered for the fish, seaweed and shellfish caught or gathered by villagers who lived *makai* or towards the sea. In this simple pattern, the land and sea provided a bounty blessed by the gods which the people learned to share. Open giving in a spirit of *aloha* was highly valued in this world, while greed or selfishness would incur the wrath of the gods.

The *ohana* or family was of central importance to the way of life in the *na kahiko*. Indeed, the *hulahula*, dances and *mele,* song of the people often told of the family genealogy of hundreds of generations begat from the mythic days of origin. Large, extended families lived within close proximity of one another, sharing labor, food, support and love. When family disputes or bitter quarrels arose, the people openly discussed their problems during *hooponopono,* sessions where ill-feelings were expressed, discussed and then set aside.

The *ohana* also nurtured the care and love of the offspring. Homes in old Hawaii which were without children were considered homes without life. Reared within the extended family, the infant was often cared for by several relatives and older siblings so that it quickly learned to adapt to a communal family system. It was not uncommon for a child to be hanai or

given to its grandparents or other close family member. Such a child was not severing its parental ties, but extending the network of kin.

The history of old Hawaii can also be experienced at Kealakekua Bay on the south Kona coast where the Hawaiian way of life dramatically changed after the arrival of Kapena Kuke or Captain James Cook in January, 1779. His ships the *Resolution* and *Discovery* caused much excitement among the Native Hawaiians, who saw them as moku or floating islands. The tall masts of the ships shrouded in white cloth miraculously resembled the high poles draped in white kapa which were used to celebrate the *Makahiki* or harvest festival in the honor of the god Lono, who in the legendary past had left Hawaii, promising one day to return. Who could deny then, that the leader of these strange men on floating islands was most assuredly this legendary god come home?

The natives marvelled at these men who travelled with Lono. Their skins were wrinkled; they had holes in their thighs; some had sparkling eyes and angular heads; others breathed fire and they all spoke a gibberish-like sputtering from their lips. Clothing, pockets, eye glasses, tri-cornered hats and pipes were new to Hawaiians. Iron metal held their island together, and they had deadly weapons the natives called waiki or spouting water. The Hawaiian *na kahiko* had been introduced to the larger world, and from that day forward, great changes would alter the people.

At the shore of Kealakekua, near the beach at Napoopoo, a restoration of the ancient temple in which Captain Cook allowed himself to be venerated as Lono can today be explored. By allowing himself to be thus honored, Cook had made a tragic mistake which would eventually lead to the unfortunate events culminating in his death. Many years after the death of Captain Cook at Kealakekua, old Hawaiians would still recall the mixture of joy, fear and awe they had first felt seeing the god Lono. When shown simple drawings of the skirmish which took the great navigator's life, they would shed tears at the memory of friends or relatives who were killed on that bloody afternoon. The white, obelisk monument that stands near the place where Kapena Kuke died is a stark symbol of the friendship and tragedy that marked the first encounter between the Hawaiian people and the foreigners who would increasingly inhabit their island kingdom.

Another great man would see his destiny unfold in the district between Ka Lae along the coast towards Kona. Even though he had been born and raised in Kohala to the north, it was in the court of his Uncle Kalaniopuu in the Kealakekua region where the great chief Kamehameha learned the arts of war and statecraft and first met Cook, who demonstrated to the young chief the power of gunpowder and firearms. It was on the battlefield of Mokuohai near Napoopoo where Kamehameha achieved his first great victory on his quest to command Hawaii and then Maui, Molokai, Lanai, Oahu, Kauai and Niihau.

As the traveller moves through this expansive district, the memories of these monumental events press upon the imagination. Time seems to roll back in remote fishing villages such as Milolii, tranquil bays like Kealakekua or the protected enclosure of Puuhonua o Honaunau or Place of Refuge. In the stone vestiges of temples, walls and monuments of this sacred, southern land, the history of the Hawaiian people is vividly revealed in tragedy and triumph.

The lonely landscape of South Point, the southern-most point in the United States, was the first landing area of the pioneer Polynesian navigators who were to settle the Hawaiian Islands. □Photo: Pat Duefrene

Green Sand Beach near South Point provides the Hawaii traveller with a wondrous sight—green tinted sand! This secluded beach is the depository of fine grains of olivine, a green volcanic stone that the ocean "mines" from a nearby littoral cone called Puu o Mahana. Although usually of a very small grain, an occasional beachcomber has found a finely polished olivine crystal of gem purity and size.   □Photo: Peter French

Ancient Hawaiian navigators developed ingenious methods for securing their *waa*, canoes, on the most foreboding of lava-covered shores despite rough waters and protruding rocks. A modern day canoe-launching device at South Point utilizes modern technology to replicate ancient skills. □Photo: Douglas Peebles

Milolii fishermen use their distinctively shaped outrigger canoes to harvest the rich bounty of the clear ocean waters off the Kona coast.
☐Photo: Peter French

The obelisk monument for Captain Cook at Kaawaloa in Kealakekua Bay was the scene of a sesquicentennial celebration in 1928. The scene of the death of the great British navigator has attracted visitors since the early nineteenth century.   □Photo: Tai Sing Loo/ Baker-Van Dyke Collection

Kaawaloa and the Cook monument appeared far differently in 1880 than it does today. The structures in this photograph are no longer standing and Kaawaloa is now covered with tall shrubs.
□Photo: Chase/ Baker-Van Dyke Collection

Native Hawaiians dressed as *alii*, chiefs and *makaainana*, commoners, reenacted first contact with Captain Cook at Kealakekua Bay during the 1928 Sesquicentennial Celebration.
□Photo: Tai Sing Loo/ Baker-Van Dyke Collection

The pageantry of the 1928 sesquicentennial of the arrival of Captain Cook in Hawaii was highlighted by the visit of a British cruiser and a U.S. Navy battleship behind the fleet of Hawaiian canoes that filled Kealakekua Bay.
□Photo: Tai Sing Loo/Baker-Van Dyke Collection

In the heyday of the inter-island steamships, Hookena landing was the scene of many arrivals as depicted in this turn-of-the-century photograph. The blend of old Hawaii and Western influences is marvelously captured in the interplay of grass and wooden houses.
☐Photo: J.A.Gonsalves/Baker-Van Dyke Collection

The southern district of Ka'u first received the knowledge of Christianity from itinerant missionaries who passed through the area, gathering small groups of Hawaiians together so as to preach the Gospel. It wasn't until 1841 with the establishment of the Kauaoha'ao Church in Waiohinu that the Congregational faith had a firm rooting in the historic lands of Ka'u.
□Photo: Greg Vaughn

Puuhonua o Honaunau, the Place of Refuge, has been a sanctuary for serenity and healing for centuries. □Photo: Peter French

A Native Hawaiian makes a sandal
in the old way at the annual Cultural
Festival hosted by the National Park
Service at Puuhonua o Honaunau.
Modern visitors will find several
ancient crafts demonstrated within
the historic religious site.
☐ Photo: Greg Vaughn

These *pohaku kii* or petroglyphs on a rock at Milolii village are carvings in stone made by ancient Hawaiians. Their meanings range from simple expressions of personal identity, to representations of the gods and observations of famous events. From the concentration of *pohaku kii* in specific locales, it is believed that their presence indicated a stone or site of intense spiritual importance. □Photo: Pat Duefrene

Sunset at Hale o Keawe in Puuhonua o Honaunau bestows a mystical quality to this sacred site.   □Photo: Nobu Nakayama

Coffee shacks and mills grace the upland above Kealakekua and
Honaunau. Initiated by Japanese and Chinese independent farmers, the coffee
industry has become one of Hawaii's important economic resources.
□Photo: Greg Vaughn

Kona Coffee

Along the mauka, upland road of the town of Captain Cook, Japanese and
Chinese immigrant coffee growers at the turn of the century could be seen
leading their ''kona nightingales,'' or donkeys laden with large sacks of the
aromatic bean. Coffee orchards from Kealakekua to Kona had become
famous through the declaration of Samuel ''Mark Twain'' Clemens that ''I
think the Kona coffee has a richer flavor than any other, be it grown where
it may and call it by what name you please.''

For the early Asian immigrants to Hawaii, Kona coffee was more than a
pleasant beverage—it was the hope for independence and success in a land
dominated by the sugar plantation. Following a three-year contract which
bound them to plantation labor, some enterprising Chinese and Japanese
workers chaffed at the low wages and long hours of sugar agriculture. With
dreams of Hawaii as a land of riches, they had hoped to make their fortunes
and return to their homeland as wealthy men. Disappointed by the sugar
plantation system, determined to make their dreams come true, some
moved to Kona to start up independent farms when their contracts expired.
On lease-hold land, these ambitious small farmers helped make the Kona
coffee industry world famous. Through their spirit of achievement, a
thriving commercial coffee business operated by small but profit-making
firms spread through the mauka Kona region.

A visit to Kealakekua would not be complete without a stop at one
of these coffee mills to sample the rich Hawaiian brew. The Kona Coffee
Festival, complete with ''kona nightingales'' in parade, has annually
honored this century-old agricultural industry begun on the island
of Hawaii.

The aromatic, shining coffee bean of Kona is the only commercially grown coffee in the United States.
☐Photo: Greg Vaughn

When the coffee tree blooms, their narrow, dark leaves are a foil for a pure white, delicately scented flower.
☐Photo: Greg Vaughn

A Royal Village: Kailua-Kona

The start of the swim competition of the Ironman Triathlon churns the waters of Kailua Bay.
☐ Photo: Greg Vaughn

CHAPTER III

A Royal Village: Kailua-Kona

The villagers of Kailua on the Kona coast of Hawaii would not soon forget the shattering events of 1819 that would forever alter the fabric of Hawaiian civilization. A place favored by Kamehameha the Great, it was at Kailua in May 8, 1819 where their beloved King died. Despite the efforts of medical *kahuna* and western friends to restore the ailing monarch's health, Kamehameha passed away to the unassuaged grief of his subjects. Without the strong leadership of this powerful chief, the native people anxiously anticipated the kingdom's new directions to be navigated by Liholiho or Kamehameha II, the sacred son of Kamehameha.

A few months later they learned the bold course the government was to follow. After being isolated north of Kailua at Kohala following his father's death, Liholiho returned to this royal village for his assumption of power. The young King, very dependent upon the advice of his mother, Keopualani and his father's favorite wife, Kaahumanu, knew that these great chiefesses had decided, with the support of high priest Hewahewa, to leap into the modern world. On the evening of his arrival at Kailua, Kamehameha II entered the public eating house where before thousands of natives and foreigners, he defied the gods of old and dared to freely eat the food of women. The *kapu* or laws of segregated eating had been broken at the encouragement of Keopualani and Kaahumanu, who were eager to free themselves from the old restrictions placed on their sex. The moment Liholiho's mouth touched the forbidden women's food, the gods had fled Hawaii and in the ensuing pandemonium the *heiau*, temples and *kii*, wooden images, were ordered destroyed and burned. In a single, dramatic moment the *na kahiko*, the old ways had perished.

In this dramatic act of defiance, the religious structure of Hawaiian civilization was officially shattered. The cycles of life that had once characterized the ancient civilization were now opened to transformation by western technology, weapons and individual choice. After 1819 the native people would face cultural chaos, increasing foreign diseases and population decline without the comfort of their old *kapu*.

It was also at Kailua a few months later where Christianity was first introduced to the Hawaiian people. Even as these unsettling events were unfolding in Hawaii, half a world away the first company of American Protestant missionaries set sail from Boston, unaware of the startling developments altering Hawaiian life. The Sandwich Islands Mission had been inspired by a Hawaiian youth, Opukahaia or Henry Obookiah who had been residing in New England. Born near Kealakekua, the young Opukahaia found himself in America after seeking adventure aboard an American ship. He was cared for by a New England family, who encouraged his conversion to Christianity. At the Cornwall Foreign Mission School in Connecticut this charismatic, forceful Hawaiian reiterated his challenging call to the idealistic New Englanders seeking an outlet for their own religious enthusiasm ''I hope the Lord will send the Gospel to the heathen land, where the words of the Savior never yet had been.'' Seven young Protestant missionary couples would answer that call. Accompanied by four Hawaiian students from the Cornwall school, this pioneer company set sail for Hawaii without Opukahaia. He had died of typhus in 1818, his dream of returning to his home to preach the Gospel stilled, his bones interred in a little grave outside of Cornwall.

The impact of Opukahaia's life and message is preserved in Mokuaikaua Church, whose white spire still dominates Kailua bay. Established as the first Christian church in 1820, Mokuaikaua Church was initially a simple thatch roof *hale pule* or house of prayer. The present-day structure, constructed out of stone in 1838, was the site of active missionary labors by Reverend Asa Thurston and his wife Lucy Thurston, who were to spend the rest of their lives in their new island home. The distinctive Mokuaikaua Church served as the religious and educational center of leeward Hawaii for several generations. By the mid-nineteenth century, through the efforts of Christianized native chiefs, teachers and their missionary tutors, the Hawaiian nation would attain a literacy rate among the highest in the world.

The changing lifestyles and religion of the Hawaiian people in these critical years is also reflected in the simple regalness of Hulihee Palace, fronting Kailua bay across from Mokuaikaua Church. Built by the Christian chief Kuakini, Hulihee Palace became a favorite summer resort for Hawaiian royalty. Open today to the public by the Daughters of Hawaii, the Palace is a treasure house of ancient *lauhala* mats made from weaving the fiber of the pandanus tree, elegant *koa* wood furniture, Hawaiian quilts and other vestiges of Hawaii's lost royal past.

As Hawaiian customs, tastes and lifestyles changed in the nineteenth century, so too did the land. In the upland country above Kailua, the introduction of extensive coffee and later macadamia nut cultivation would replace the earlier patterns of Hawaiian agriculture. Japanese and Chinese farmers, eager to escape the rigors and poor pay of the sugar plantation, had moved to the Kona district by the 1890's and began to plant coffee in the cooler uplands. Thus was born what would become a world renown enterprise, the Kona coffee industry, the only coffee grown commercially on American soil.

The story of macadamia nuts commenced in 1881 when W. H. Purvis planted a pocketful of the nuts at Honokaa, a village on the Hamakua Coast. Named for Dr. John Macadam, a botanist and amateur chef who popularized the nut in Queensland, the hard macadamia nut posed a unique challenge to commercial farmers—how to crack the outer shell without crushing the meat. That question was answered in 1939 when a nut-cracking machine finally made the process profitable. From Ka'u to Kona to Honokaa, the macadamia nut tree has now become a familiar commercial crop on the Hawaii terrain.

In its past, then, Kailua has long been a setting for change as new trends were assimilated into island life. Modern Kailua-Kona perpetuates this tradition as one of the fastest developing areas in Hawaii. Kona's warm and sunny climate has made Kona a mecca for visitors and new residents from around the world. Luxurious hotels have been developed at Keauhou beach, south of Kailua, serving the increasing number of vacationers, snorkelers, sports lovers, deep-sea marlin fishing enthusiasts and those who simply seek the beauty and history of old Hawaii.

Kailua Bay has retained the beauty of its natural ocean ambience even though it has become one of the fastest growing commercial, residential and visitor centers on the Big Island. ☐ Photo: Greg Vaughn

A Kona wedding chapel and garden indicate that one of the increasingly important sources of tourism for Hawaii is from Japan. Young Japanese couples journey to Kona to be married in these idyllic settings.
☐Photo: Peter French

The golf course of The Kona Country Club surrounding The Kona Surf Resort provides the public with an excellent golfing facility.
☐Photo: Greg Vaughn

Romance in Kona

Western marriages began as a tradition in Kona at Mokuaikaua Church where missionary Reverend Asa Thurston performed countless ceremonies between Native Hawaiian men and women who had been Christianized and Western *haole*, foreigners and native women. While Kamehameha the Great had many wives, with the advent of Christian influences monogamy became the law and custom by mid-century.

The number of inter-racial marriages in port towns such as Kona were numerous in that century. When Isabella Bird visited Kona in 1873, she noted that most of the white men were married to native women, "and are rearing a dusky race, of children who speak the maternal tongue only, and grow up with native habits." These white men, she further noted, seem "infatuated by the ease and lusciousness of this languid region." While the current day Japanese newlyweds return to their country after a whirlwind Big Island marriage and honeymoon, the romance on the Kona shores remains unforgettable.

The Royal Kona provides its guests with a sumptuous nighttime *luau* in the royal tradition. ☐ Photo: Greg Vaughn

The Keiki Hula Festival displays the charm and skill at Hawaiian dance of the Big Island's beloved children. ☐Photo: Peter French

Accompanied by their pink-clad elders, the *keiki* or children demonstrate that the *hula* knows no age.
☐Photo: Peter French

A young dancer, be-decked in neck and head *lei*, smiles for the camera during the Keiki Hula Festival.
☐Photo: Greg Vaughn

A Hawaiian outrigger canoe cuts across Kailua Bay as a rainbow blesses the town with beauty and good fortune.
☐Photo: Greg Vaughn

The dusty, quiet town of Kona at the turn of the century appeared as a lazy Pacific village in this 1908 photograph. This view of the main street was taken near the site of the future Kona Inn.   □Photo: Baker-Van Dyke Collection

Old Kona

Kona today is one of the fasting growing communities in Hawaii. The dry, sunny weather and beautiful oceanfront have made Kona a favorite vacation spot for sunbathers, fishermen and water sports enthusiasts worldwide. Commercial industries have relocated to Kona, as have an increasing number of retirees who have found the predictable weather far more suitable to their golden years than their original mainland homes. In the next few decades, the future of Kona will be rewritten by these new economic and social winds of change.

But a stroll along the main street of Kona, despite the hustle-and-bustle of visitors, joggers or fishermen, can still be a walk into the Kona of old, when donkeys and carriages not automobiles dominated the dusty lanes. The steeple of Hawaii's first Christian church, Mokuaikaua still retains its

prominence, as does the regal gate of Hulihee Palace along the oceanfront. The tree lined thoroughfare along the seawall, laced with clusters of palms, still evokes the tropical paradise that was described by Isabella Bird in 1873 as ''a land where all things always seem the same,'' or ''truly a region of endless afternoons.'' Rich in forests, vegetation and gentle winds, old Kona's even climate created a life so quiet that ''people speak in hushed, thin voices, and move as in a lethargy, dreaming too!''

At the turn of the century, Kona served as one small port village on the west Hawaii coast along with Kawaihae to the north and Kealakekua and Hookena to the south. In those days, visitors were rare so Kona needed only one regular boarding house. ''The company is accidental and promiscuous,'' Miss Bird noted of this boarding house. ''The conversation

Twenty-five years later Kona village was still relatively quiet. This 1933 aerial view shows the steeple of Mokuaikaua Church, American Factors sheds and the site of Ahuena Heiau on the point in the foreground.
□Photo: Baker-Van Dyke Collection

consists of speculations, varied and repeated with the hours, as to the arrivals and departures of the Honolulu schooners . . . who they will bring, who they will take, and how long their respective passages will be. A certain amount of local gossip is also hashed up at each meal, and every stranger who has traveled through Hawaii for the last ten years is picked to pieces and worn threadbare, and his purse, weight, entertainers, and habits are thoroughly canvassed.''

Idle chatter and gossip helped pass the hours in this Pacific village where Polynesian lifestyles had blended with the strong American influences to produce a special way of life in Hawaii. Sunday, of course, was kept strictly solemn with no work, no business, no cooking, and no frivolous amusements allowed. The missionary influence under the ministry of Reverend Asa Thurston had helped maintain a deep-seated Sabbath devotion. The churches would be filled on Sundays with Hawaiians in their best clothes, singing in their native language the most beautiful hymns and prayers. Foreign visitors frequently noted that the Hawaiian people were among the most devout and adoring Christians they had ever met.

Such was the easy, loving tempo of life in old Kona. It takes but little imagination to recall those yesterdays when donkeys filled the streets, chatter was long-winded, Sundays were kept pious and the summer seemed endless and unchanging.

Hulihee Palace, located on Kailua Bay, recalls Kona's royal past.
☐ Photo: Greg Vaughn

Hulihee Palace

When Hawaiian royalty of the nineteenth century journeyed to Kona, they stayed in elegant style in the two-storied, white columned home known as Hulihee Palace. Constructed across the road from Mokuaikaua Church and fronting the cooling winds of Kailua Bay, Hulihee was originally the home of Christian chief Kuakini. Born in 1791 at Kahaluu on Hawaii, Kuakini was a chief of double royal paternity which greatly elevated his prestige. Described by the historian Samuel M. Kamakau as a ''fine-looking man with a proud carriage and a handsome rosy face,'' he was also a powerful man of immense size (he weighed over four hundred pounds). As Governor of Hawaii under the Kamehameha government, he was recognized as a stern enforcer of law. The Governor was commonly called John Adams by foreigners—a nickname he personally chose after the second President of the United States.

Under the direction of Kuakini, the stone Makuaikaua Church was built in the 1830s, as well as the fine wooden house in 1837-38 that was called Hulihee Palace. At nine o'clock on the morning of December 9, 1844, he died at Hulihee. The Palace remained in the hands of the royal families, lending comfort to visiting monarchs such as King Kalakaua near the end of the century.

Currently under the care of the Daughters of Hawaii, Hulihee Palace is open to the public for tours. Some of the finest collections of koa bowls and kapa, Hawaiian artifacts, Victorian and Chinese pearl-inlaid furniture are exhibited in the gracious Palace rooms. The Polynesian, Asian and Eastern blends of culture that embody the history of Hawaii are reflected in the history of Hawaii's royal palace.

Reconstructed under the auspices of the King Kamehameha Hotel,
Ahuena Heiau was a historic temple where Kamehameha the Great
worshipped in the years before his death.   □Photo: Greg Vaughn

Ahuena Heiau

After his long struggle to unify the Hawaiian islands into a single kingdom, Kamehameha the Great frequently visited Kailua, eventually establishing his last royal court there. In his remaining years, the king spent much of his time at Kailua rebuilding heiau, including the temple of Ahuena at the northern point of the bay. With great effort, tall images were carved out of ohia wood with grinning mouths, elongated heads with helmets, rounded thighs and legs, and below the feet a block of wood to plant in the ground. As the Hawaiian historian Samuel M. Kamakau explained, ''These carved images were not objects of worship; the people did not kneel to them, nor did the kahunas worship them.'' Rather than objects of veneration, ''they were made for decoration to make the god house handsome and attractive to the god when he came from heaven.'' Evidently, they were not necessarily considered sacred. ''At times,'' S. M.

Kamakau explains, ''they were used by the people who kept the houses of the gods to fire the cook's ovens.''

At the age of 83 years old (according to S.M. Kamakau), Kamehameha the Great died at Kailua on May 8, 1819. Within a year, the Hawaiian religion of which he was a firm believer would be overthrown, the temples and idols ordered burned. Like other sacred sites, Ahuena temple was abandoned, its stone foundation left as a remnant of the ancient traditions. Thanks to a restoration effort by the King Kamehameha Hotel, Ahuena Heiau has been re-created. Its powerful, dramatic structures and images recall the era when Kamehameha the Great, worshiping his god Kukailimoku, had conquered the island realm, established a single rule of chiefs, and brought peace and prosperity to the land.

Hawaiian *kii* or images such as this modern reproduction at Ahuena Heiau were destroyed in 1819 following the lifting of the ancient *kapu* by Liholiho, Kamehameha II.
Photo: Greg Vaughn

A team of *wahine* or women paddlers race from Kailua to Honaunau in their outrigger canoe. Once the exclusive sport of *kane* or men, female canoe teams have been organized throughout modern Hawaii.
□Photo: Greg Vaughn

Bikers take the first turn during the Ironman Triatholon competition in Kona.
☐Photo: Peter French

The finish line is crossed in what is called one of the sporting world's most grueling tests of human endurance.
☐Photo: Greg Vaughn

Kona and the Ironman

The Bud Light Ironman Triatholon World Championship of Kona is not for the faint-hearted. The competition begins with a 2.4 mile ocean swim in the waters of Kailua-Kona, followed by a 112 mile bicycle race from Kona to Hawi in Kohala. If that were not enough, the competitors then must complete a 26.2 mile marathon run along the Kona Coast. It is a race fit for the very strongest or the most insane of men and women.

Actually, there are now so many of these daring competitors gathering from around the world in Kona to test their skills in the Triatholon, that a lottery is required to determine who can enter the competition. What began as a whimsical idea among naval Commander John Collins and a few friends in a Waikiki bar, is now one of the most publicized sporting competitions in the world. The first race was conducted in 1978 on Oahu under the direction of Commander Collins. By 1982, the race was being conducted in Kona under the sponsorship of Bud Light. In the grand tradition of Native Hawaiians who honored physical prowess and competition, the Ironman Triatholon has become a permanent attraction in Kona.

A bicyclist races against the setting sun in the Ironman
Triatholon. ☐Photo: Peter French

A winning marlin in Kona's International Billfish Tournament is proudly displayed between its pursuer and a Kona beauty queen.
□Photo: Greg Vaughn

A marlin is weighed-in during the Billfish Tournament. It requires many hours of patience, but the snaring of a mighty Kona billfish is a thrilling, incomparable experience. □Photo: Greg Vaughn

International Billfish Tournament

Every August, Kona comes alive with fishing teams from around the world, each of them eager to capture the top prizes in the International Billfish Tournament. About 75 teams from as far as Australia and the Bahamas converge for a week on this village known for the abundance, size and fight of its marlin.

The competition, based on teams of anglers, involves a complex scoring system that emphasizes skill as well as pure weight of the catch. First, only a catch of over one hundred pounds will quality, with one point given for each pound of the fish. If the fish is caught on a light, 24 kilogram line, there are 33.3 bonus points. In addition, there is a 100 point bonus for the heaviest billfish caught for the day, the heaviest in the tournament and for any fish weighing 500 pounds or more.

Women have also entered the annual competition since 1959 when one day was set aside for women anglers. In 1960, twenty-one women entered the competition, with Pat Peacock of Kona taking the honors with a world record, 540-pound marlin caught on a 130 pound line.

Winners and losers of the International Billfish Tournament are not only noted for their angling talents, but their ability to party. A week of happy hours and *luau* is topped with a ceremonial banquet for presentation of awards and the "Crying Towel" for the one that got away. The annual festivities highlight the fact that Kona has emerged as one of the world's great water sport capitals.

Matching *aloha* wear on island visitors illustrates that the dry, sunny climate of Kona has made it one of the fasting growing visitor industry centers on the island of Hawaii.
□Photo: Bob Fewell

Kiholo Bay, which stretches for two miles north of Kona, contains the cool waters of a huge, spring-fed pond called Luahinewai. Water enthusiasts find the one pebble and three black sand beaches along Kiholo Bay are good places for deep water swimming during normal ocean conditions.
□Photo: Greg Vaughn

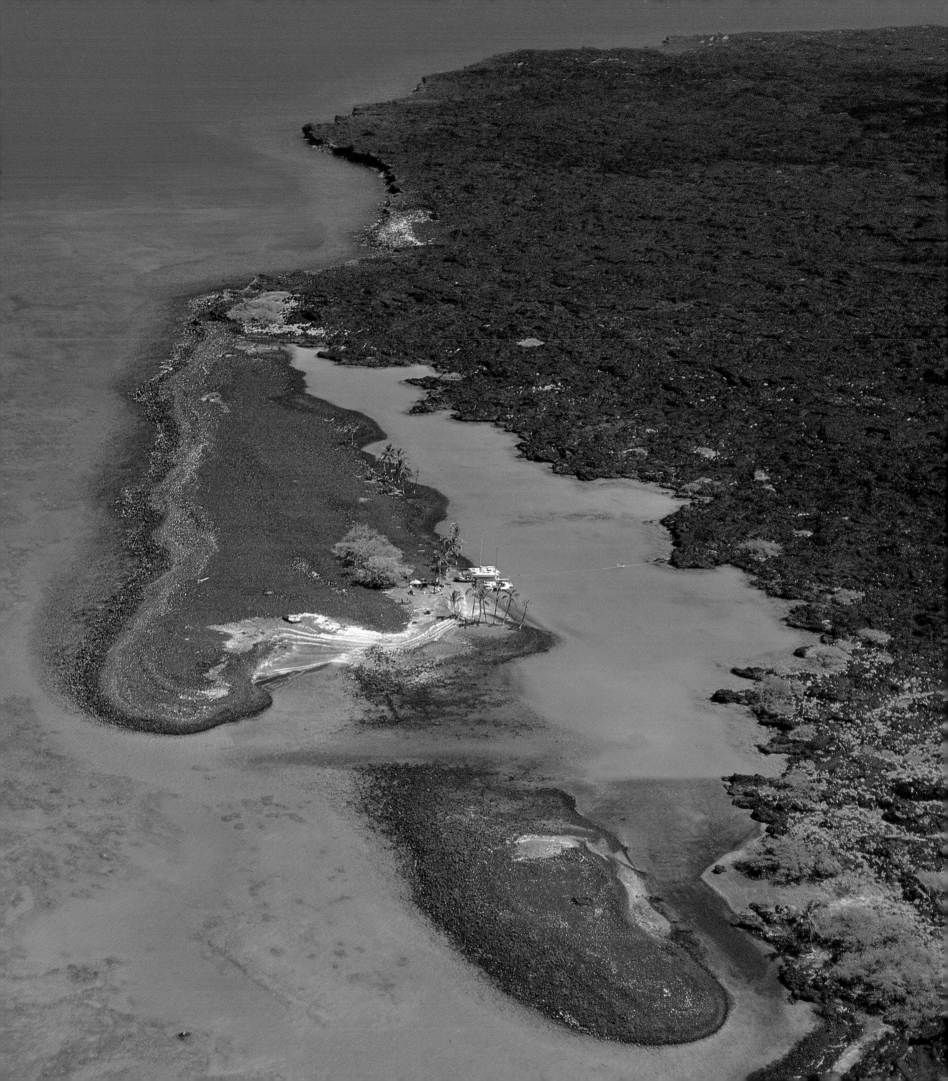

The Kona Village Resort is a tropical paradise with each of its 115 thatch-roofed cottages located on the ocean or secluded in the historic lagoon area. Coats and ties are forbidden. Visitors can indulge in sailing, outrigger canoe rides, snorkeling, glass-bottom boat excursions, guided history and nature walks, *luau*, craft demonstrations, hula lessons, tennis, and swimming in one of the resort's two oceanside swimming pools.   □Photo: Peter French

The thatched houses on the lagoon at the Kona Village Resort provide Hawaiian-style life in a most comfortable fashion. □Photo: Greg Vaughn

An evening *luau* at the Kona Village Resort follows in the tradition of Hawaiian royalty who once feasted along the historic coast of North Kona. □Photo: Greg Vaughn

Along the King's Trail: The Kohala Coast

Anaehoomalu Bay at sunset is distinguished by the extensive coconut grove that fringes two fishponds and a long, curving white sand beach. Anaehoomalu is one of the most exquisite beaches on the Kohala Coast.
□ Photo: Peter French

CHAPTER IV

Along the King's Trail: The Kohala Coast

For hundreds of years Hawaiian travelers crossed the lava fields north of Kailua, moving to and from the village of Kawaihae in the Kohala district. In this dry, temperate region, blessed with beautiful white sand beaches, cool ponds and protected coves, the travelers enjoyed the bounty of the ocean and the pleasures of the surf. At special spiritual sites they carved their *pohaku kii* or petroglyphs in the stone, leaving for future generations a permanent record of their journey. In time the path these countless men and women walked became packed under their feet as a shiny lava road known as Ala Mamalahoa or as it is called today, the ''King's Trail.''

A journey along this historic path today would reveal a unique and attractive blend of yesterday and tomorrow. The nine miles of the Kohala Coast from Anaehoomalu Bay in the south to Kawaihae still is characterized by the expansive, rugged lava fields of prehistory, the beaches of quiet splendor and the ancient sites of the Hawaiian people such as the impressive temple, Puukohola. Yet through irrigation and imaginative development, modern oases have been created along this coast. With nearly two billion dollars scheduled to be invested in resort development by the year 2000, this sun-filled region has deservedly earned the title ''Gold Coast.'' Many world renowned five-star resorts and their elegant properties offer visitors and residents an unforgettable and experience in the grand tradition of Hawaiian hospitality and aloha.

The Kohala Coast resorts are especially famous for the compulsive beauty of the neighboring ocean. As the visitor soon discovers, the Hawaiian sea is a source of delicious food, refreshing comfort, quiet contemplation or exciting recreation. The modern day resorts have carefully integrated their location, design and accommodations to the rhythms of the sea and the opportunities it offers for human comfort and adventure.

The modern ocean explorer follows in the tradition of the ancient Hawaiians who studied *ka moana* or the ocean closely, and revered it in their religion, art, song, food and wars. One of the most important uses of the sea was as a source for food. The Hawaiians method of fishing was a highly developed art with religious overtones. Before a day of fishing, the men would gather in the evening in the *kuula heiau* or fishing temple bringing with them their nets, sleeping apparel, pigs, bananas, coconuts and *poi* that they might spend the night and worship the god of fishing. In the morning they would fish along the shore by hand or even use spears. Hooks were fashioned from a variety of materials including human bone, tortoise shell and the bones of pigs and dogs. The deep water *opelu* or *aku* were caught from canoe, while fishnets were used to surround large schools of fish near shore. The turtle, lobster and *manini* fish were obtained by diving.

The Hawaiians of old not only caught their fish in the sea, but harvested them in offshore and inland fishponds, remnants of which can still be seen along the Kohala Coast. Spawning and nurturing the fish within these cleverly designed areas, fish such as mullet were fattened for food.

Fishing was regulated by signs, omens, and the will of the gods. When a Hawaiian family journeyed from Waimea to Kawaihae to fish, they would be careful never to mention their destination or purpose. ''The fish have ears and will hide,'' the youngsters were told. Winds from the mountain or from the sea told the fisherman what kind of fish could be caught and offerings were made at the fish shrines that were common along the shore. Knowledge of good offshore fishing areas was carefully guarded and the amount of fish taken carefully controlled. Hawaiians were strict conservationists, enforcing closed seasons on fish and plant life so that the bounty of the sea could be continually replenished.

The Hawaiian Pacific ridge which surrounds the chain of islands underlies a watery region teeming with vegetation and marine life that to the modern day diver remains an azure world of incandescent hues, colorful tropical fish and exotic seaweed. The snorkeler in Kohala waters enters a submarine world that is a wonderment of coral, eels, fishes, plant life and invertebrates. At depths of one hundred meters and more, precious pink and gold corals are discovered as well as the bivalve *pinna* bottom-dwelling forms which live where there is little or no light and which maintain themselves on detritus and plankton falling through the water. The coastline is lined with rocky shores and tide pools, calcareous beaches, fringing and subtidal coral reefs and sandy coasts. The Pacific ocean around Hawaii teems with life. There are over 700 species of fish existing at various depths, 400 seaweeds and algae, 1,000 types of mollusk, and 1,350 species of invertebrates in the shallow waters around the islands.

The ocean not only provides an abundance of food and nourishment, but an important source of recreation. It was the ancient Hawaiian who perfected the art of surfing and excelled at swimming, diving, paddling and sailing. The natural enjoyment of these water sports is well understood by anyone who has experienced the thrill of ''riding the curl'' of an advancing wave on a long, lean surfboard or has felt the exhilaration of a outrigger canoe race.

Through the efforts of the world-class Kohala Coast resorts, the adventure offered by Hawaii's ocean is being made more readily available to increasing numbers of visitors and residents. Developed beaches have created a new vista of relaxation as fishing, water sports, golfing, sightseeing, horseback riding, discovering Hawaiian history and quiet relaxation along the ''King's Trail'' provides lasting satisfaction to a myriad of interests. It is not uncommon for some chefs in the resorts' restaurants to spend their mornings diving in the nearby sea so as to put fresh crustaceans upon the evening table.

After having journeyed the length of the Kohala Coast and indulging in its pleasures, the visitor will most assuredly join Victorian visitor Isabella Bird who once mused: ''I delight in Hawaii more than ever, with its unconventional life, great upland sweeps, unexplored forests, riotous breezes, and general atmosphere of freedom, airiness, and expansion.'' On the Kohala Coast, those words are timeless.

Ala Mamalahoa or the "Kings Trail" is an ancient, foot-worn path that once traversed the Kohala Coast. This portion of the path, called the "Ellis Trail," was named after early Big Island visitor, Reverend William Ellis who in 1823 walked its length. ☐Photo: Peter French

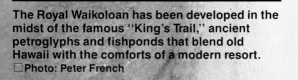

The Royal Waikoloan has been developed in the midst of the famous "King's Trail," ancient petroglyphs and fishponds that blend old Hawaii with the comforts of a modern resort.
☐ Photo: Peter French

The Anchialine Pond Preserve at The Royal Waikoloan Resort illustrates the importance of the ocean to life on the lava covered Kohala Coast.
☐Photo: Greg Vaughn

Hawaiian petroglyphs can be observed at Anaehoomalu Bay near the Royal Waikoloan Resort.   □Photo: Greg Vaughn

Anaehoomalu Bay

At Anaehoomalu Bay, between the beach and the Waikoloan Resort, are two ancient fishponds, Kuualii and Kahapapa. Once reserved for the exclusive use of Hawaiian royalty, they had been maintained and stocked with mullet by native fishermen for the delight of traveling alii who passed through the region. Anaehoomalu literally means ''reserved mullet.''

Fishponds represent a form of ''aquaculture industry'' which reached a level of complexity and skill among the ancient Hawaiians that still serves as a model to modern aquaculturalists. Especially on the islands of Kauai, Oahu and Molokai, the construction of shoreline fishponds for the purposes of harvesting fish was a skilled technique that provided an abundance of seafood. Sometimes reputed to have been constructed in a single night by the race of mythical small people called menehune, the fishponds were designed for the circulation of water without allowing the fish to escape. On the island of Hawaii, they were less frequent except along the western coast.

The striking, white beaches of Anaehoomalu Bay that slope gradually into deeper waters offshore, provided Hawaiians with an abundant source of fish and recreation. Swimming, snorkeling, scuba diving, net-fishing, wind-surfing and sometimes surfing can be enjoyed in these waters year-round. Between the fishponds and ocean resources, the visiting alii who passed through Anaehoomalu Bay were given comforts befitting their station.

Oceanfront along the Kohala Coast, Hilton Waikoloa Village blends contemporary facilities with graceful Hawaiian culture to create a resort unlike any other. Guests can enjoy lush tropical landscaping, waterfalls, a mile-long museum walkway, wildlife, three freshwater pools (one pictured here), a swimming/snorkeling saltwater lagoon and beach, the Dolphin Quest Learning Center, 8 tennis courts, two 18-hole golf courses, and the Kohala Spa. 1,240 spacious guest rooms and suites in three low-rise towers are connected via waterways traversed by twelve mahogany canal boats or two Swiss-made trams.
□ Hilton Waikoloa Village

The Hilton Waikoloa Village is a fantasy of lights in the tropical evening. ☐ Photos: Peter French

It is not surprising that the architecture and landscaping on the Kohala Coast is becoming internationally known for their elegance and uniqueness. The beauty of both the structures and surrounding grounds are particularly apparent at dusk when lengthening shadows and glowing light of the setting sun become additional visible elements. Upscale private residents as well as the resorts are deliberately planned to incorporate the natural environment with distinct design elements and materials. Likewise the grounds of the resorts blend local foliage and tropical elements into a harmonious setting with the man-made additions.
☐Photo above: Lee Allen Thomas   ☐Photo right: Peter French

The man-made physical environments of the Kohala Coast's magnificent resorts often equal the splendor of nature. Here a dolphin is enjoying his new habitat in the dolphin lagoon at the Hilton Waikoloa Village.   ☐Photo: Scott Rutherford

The Mauna Lani Bay Hotel and Bungalows is located amid ancient fishponds, twenty-seven acres of important historic sites and one of the Kohala Coast's most beautiful beaches. Offering 354 rooms, the hotel's outstanding amenities include ten tennis courts, an eighteen-hole golf course, health spa, swimming pool, ocean activities, two lounges and four restaurants—two of them award winners. □Photo: Peter French

The sixth hole of the Mauna Lani Resort Golf Course offers excellent golfing and a breathtaking view.
□ Photo: Greg Vaughn

Hopeala fishpond in the Mauna Lani Resort is still an active, functioning example of Hawaiian aquaculture.
☐ Photo: Greg Vaughn

A catamaran cruise passes offshore from the Mauna Lani Resort on the Kohala Coast. ☐Photo: Greg Vaughn

Catamaran enthusiasts launch off a Kohala Beach for a thrilling day of testing the currents, tides and winds of the Pacific Ocean.
☐Photo: Lee Allen Thomas

The award-winning Orchid at Mauna Lani is nestled on 32 beachfront acres on the sunny Kohala Coast. Here, tastefully-appointed interiors complement the beauty of the island's natural surroundings. From world-class golf to scuba diving, horseback riding to hiking a volcano, beach boys program to "Spa Without Walls,"—the recreational possibilities are as diverse as the island itself. Free-form swimming pool, tidal pool whirlpools, white sand lagoon, ten tennis courts, shopping, and more. Exquisite dining. Warm island hospitality and unsurpassed service. □The Orchid at Mauna Lani

Hapuna Beach, over half a mile long and in the summer 200 feet deep, is the widest white sand beach on the Big Island. Known for its excellent board and body-surfing, Hapuna is also a place for *lelekawa*, the Hawaiian sport of diving from sea cliffs feet first, making the least possible splash. ☐ Photo: Peter French

Hapuna Beach State Recreation Area has in recent years become the Big Island's most popular beach area with users driving all the way from Hilo and Puna. ☐Photo: Nobu Nakayama

Golfing on luxurious greens, surrounded by palm trees and the impressive Hualalai volcano in the background can be eden on earth for the golfing enthusiast. □Photo: Lee Allen Thomas

The Mauna Kea Beach Hotel is situated on one of the most beautiful beaches in Hawaii. Blending in with its environment of sand, sea, and volcanic mountains, the hotel's terraced architecture offers privacy and unobstructed views. The many worlds of Mauna Kea include the challenge of a Robert Trent Jones, Sr. golf course, 13 ocean-front tennis courts, water sports, and numerous other diversions—the perfect complement to the finest in accommodations and service. □Mauna Kea Beach Hotel

This aerial view of Four Seasons Resort shows the bird's-eye perspective of the five crescents which afford each guest an ocean view from their lanai. The beach tree pool, which lies just a few feet from the lapping Pacific Ocean, offers a tranquil setting to relax and rejuvenate.

The ancient coral reefs off Kawaihae are stunningly beautiful in the clear Pacific water as seen from a helicopter from Kona Helicopters, Inc.   ☐Photo: Lee Allen Thomas

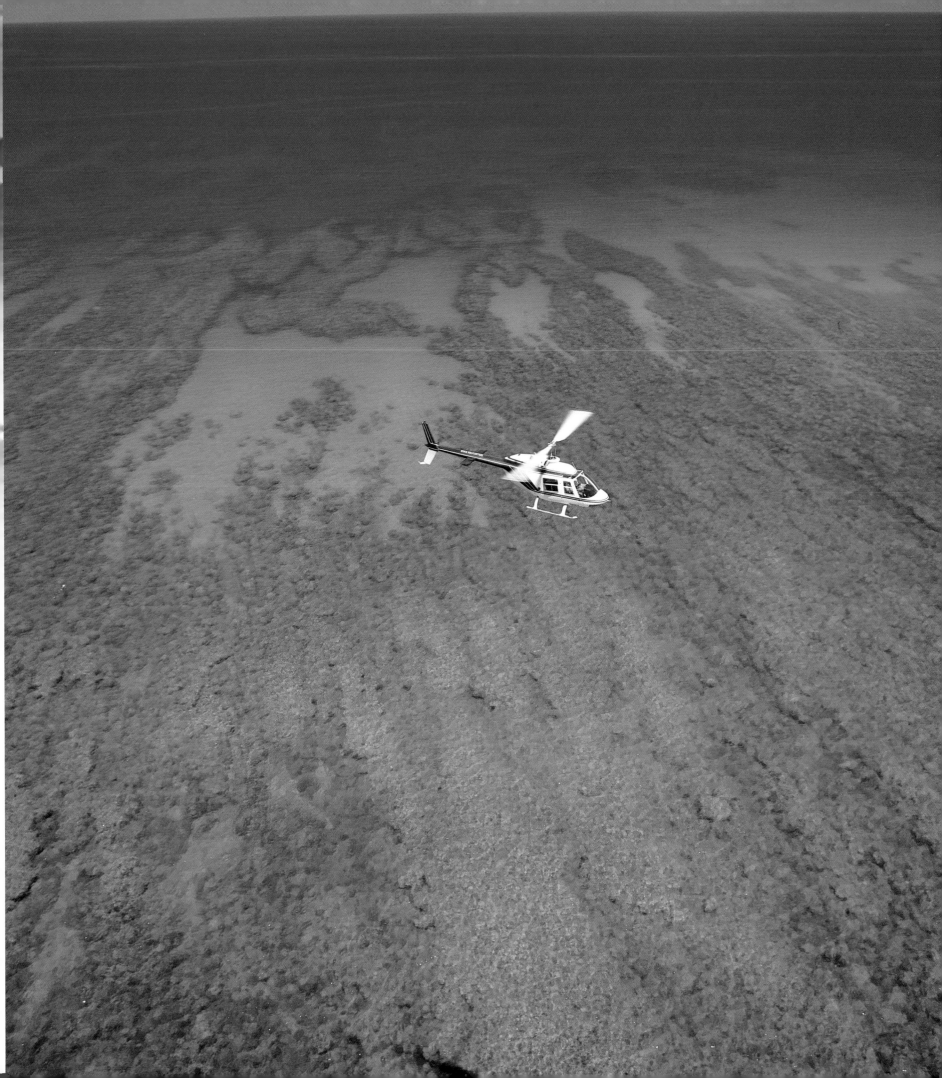

Wind-surfing has become a new island sport, combining the thrill of sailing with the ancient surfing sport of the Hawaiian people. □Photo: Nobu Nakayama

At Kawaihae, cattle were tied to the sides of whale boats by paniola, Hawaiian cowboys, for the passage to the small steamship offshore which transported the beef to markets in Honolulu. □Photo: Baker-Van Dyke Collection

In 1890, one of the sons of Reverend Lorenzo Lyons photographed the old Hokuloa Church and meeting house at Puako that his father founded in 1859. The church structure still stands as evidence of the early missionary efforts on the Kohala Coast. □Photo: Albert Lyons/Baker-Van Dyke Collection

Puukohola Heiau looms over Kawaihae Bay in this 1886 photograph of the last Hawaiian temple. The unidentified men in the foreground stand near a simple fishing hut of a much later date than the massive temple. □Photo: Bishop Museum

Puukohola Heiau

In 1791, Kamehameha ordered the construction of Puukohola Heiau on the advice of Kapoukahi, a kahuna from Kauai. This powerful priest had predicted that if Kamehameha built this temple on the hill at Kawaihae called Puukohola in honor of the war god Kukailimoku, the great warrior from Kohala would successfully unify the islands. Workers were enlisted to carry the stones of the temple from the distant northern valley of Pololu, with Kamehameha himself joining in the labor. The temple was dedicated to Kukailimoku with human sacrifices, and Kamehameha soon after led a successful assault against the island of Maui, defeating the armies of Kahekili. On Oahu, Kamehameha defeated his enemies in 1795 after a stunning though bloody victory at the battle of Nuuanu. It was said that the armies of Kalanikupule on Oahu preferred death to capture and there-fore leaped off the Nuuanu Pali rather than be taken captive by Kamehameha.

Following the conquest of Oahu, religious and military preparations were made for an invasion of Kauai and Niihau against the armies of chief Kaumualii. On one invasion attempt, storm-tossed seas made the passage of the channel impossible for Kamehameha's war canoes. Another assault was prevented in 1804 when the armies of Kamehameha were striken with a terrible disease called okuu. Finally in 1810, through a series of nego-tiations, Kaumualii peacefully ceded the islands of Kauai and Niihau to Kamehameha with the right to retain his governorship. The prophecy of Kapoukahi made at Puukohola Heiau had been fulfilled. The islands had at last been unified, establishing the lasting fame of Kamehameha.

The serene beauty of a Hawaiian *hula* girl from Hilo is captured in this 1900's portrait. □Photo: Rice and Perkins/Baker-Van Dyke Collection

The People of the Big Island

A Hawaiian student in the Hilo Boarding School in 1899 proudly poses for a graduation photograph.   □Photo: J.T.Silva/Baker-Van Dyke Collection

A Hawaiian woman sits with her child and dog on the beach at Napoopoo
in 1924.   □Photo: Ray Jerome Baker/Baker-Van Dyke Collection

CHAPTER VI   *An Island of Many Nations:*
The People of the Big Island

A "Kona nightingale" bearing a youthful load pauses near a "modern" car on a Big Island road.   □Photo: Ray Jerome Baker/Baker-Van Dyke Collection

The people of the Big Island are best understood where they are most comfortable—in their homes, among their friends or at the many celebrations where they mark the cycles of their lives. On a Saturday afternoon, in little villages such as Waiohinu, Hookena or Hawi, a small group of men may be seen waiting to open up the underground *imu* or oven in preparation for the evening *luau* or feast. One of the *keiki* or children may be celebrating their first year birthday or a teenaged nephew may be graduating from high school or grandparents may be honoring their silver anniversary. Nearly everyone in the small communities will join in the gaiety.

An elderly Portuguese man has let them use his *imu* and the men all sit in his backyard sharing beer and stories. Some of them are Hawaiian, others are Japanese, Chinese or Portuguese. Nearly all of them have a mixture of race in their blood. Occasionally one of the men stirs a large pot of a reddish liquid boiling over an open fire. When a "greenhorn" *haole* visitor asks what they are cooking, they all laugh. The innards of the pig taste best, they explain, when boiled in its own blood. It is an old Hawaii custom and the newcomer is offered to taste the rare treat, which he politely declines. The laughter is uproariously good-natured.

What is most memorable of the island men, besides their warmth and

The *keiki o ka aina*, children of the land, have a natural affinity for the beach and sea. □Photo: Ray Jerome Baker/Bishop Museum

wit, are their hands—strong, brown hands that have weathered time and yet still look as if they could wield a cane knife, rope cattle, build a massive lava stone wall or tow a net filled with fish to shore. They have lived their entire lives on the land and their hands have been shaped by the earth and the sea from which they take their living. Their hands gesture freely as they ''talk story'' about their adventures of hunting and fishing and the legends and mysterious forces that cling to their district. The afternoon slowly dissolves into sunset as the stories and beer flow more freely.

These are island people, and their lifestyles are repeated wherever the races of Hawaii intermingle, whether in Waiohinu, Kohala, Waipio or in the town of Hilo. Polynesians, Westerners and Asians, representing most every nationality and race have in the last two hundred years settled amicably in the Hawaiian Islands. While their interactions were not always peaceful or free from animosity, the spirit of *aloha* has prevailed forging a multi-cultural ''local'' island identity.

The first people to Hawaii created the aura of *aloha* which subsequent visitors learned to adopt. The ancient Hawaiians who immigrated to this north Pacific archipelago in the fourth and fifth centuries A.D. came to Hawaii from the Marquesas Islands and then later from Tahiti, travelling thousands of miles in double-hulled canoes. Their earliest settlements were on the island of Hawaii, at Ka Lae or South Point. For a thousand years they had very little contact with the outside world, developing an intricate civilization utilizing the limited resources of an island and living in harmony with nature.

Following the introduction of Hawaii in 1778 to the Western world through the expeditions of Captain James Cook, the ''Sandwich Islands'' as they were then commonly called, became a favorite seaport for merchants, sandalwood traders, whalers and common seamen from around the world. Frenchmen, Spaniards, Russians, Englishmen and Americans often escaping civilization jumped ship in the islands and settled as farmers, merchants and eventually landowners.

The Chinese were among the early foreign settlers to make Hawaii their home. As early as 1787, Chinese were coming to Hawaii on foreign ships, sometimes as cooks or seamen. Some Chinese merchants established small businesses in island ports while others developed rice or coffee farms in Waipio Valley or Kona. They also freely intermarried with Hawaiian women, thus establishing many Chinese-Hawaiian dynasties that have survived until today.

One of the more influential groups of foreigners to have settled in the Hawaiian islands were the first Protestant missionaries who arrived in

Three young Japanese girls adorned in traditional *kimono*, probably the American-born children of Japanese immigrant parents, stare wistfully into the camera.
□Photo: Rice and Perkins/Baker-Van Dyke Collection

When missionary couple Reverend Asa Thurston and Lucy Goodale Thurston arrived with the first company of Protestant missionaries in 1820, they were young, idealistic proselytizers of the Gospel. Nearly half a century later, they were photographed as the grand old couple of Mokuaikaua Church in Kona. □Photo: 1859 Ambrotype of Hugo Stangenwald/Baker-Van Dyke Collection

The family of Reverend David Belden Lyman and Sarah Joiner Lyman, missionaries stationed in Hilo, would become one of the larger and more influential clans on the Big Island.
□Photo: c. 1856: Daguerreotype of Hugo Stangenwald/Baker-Van Dyke Collection

1820 at Kawaihae on the island of Hawaii. Between the years 1820-1863 when the Protestant mission was actively spreading *palapala* and *pule,* learning and prayer, among Hawaiian natives, nearly one hundred and ninety American men and women dedicated their lives to ''fill the habitable parts of those important islands with schools and churches, fruitful fields, and pleasant dwellings.''

One hundred years after the arrival of Captain Cook the Hawaiian people had, through a tragic decline in population, become a minority in their own land. At the time of Cook's visit in 1778, there may have been a total of three hundred fifty to four hundred thousand Hawaiians throughout the inhabited island chain. In 1873 that number had been reduced by disease and cultural despair to about forty-nine thousand native people. The Big Island's population that year numbered a total of only sixteen thousand natives and foreigners.

The large sugar plantations which by the 1870's had come to dominate the Hawaiian economy offered a daring solution to the native population decline. King Kalakaua, recognizing that an infusion of new blood would help preserve his race, actively supported foreign labor immigration from Japan. Japanese would not only prove to be excellent plantation laborers, but, Kalakaua hoped, would marry native women and thus propagate the dying race.

The first Japanese immigrants arrived in 1885 and were soon placed on Big Island plantations. They were followed by literally waves of tens of thousands of other such single men seeking out a fast fortune in a land they called ''heaven.'' By 1900 over forty per cent of the population would be Japanese. On the Big Island they settled in areas such as Puna, Olaa, Hamakua coast, Honokaa, Kohala, Ka'u and Kona. The mark left by the Japanese immigrant was indelible on the Hawaiian landscape from their language schools, Buddhist temples and unique foods to their celebrations and annual festivals. Unfortunately for King Kalakaua's dream of rebuilding the native race, single Japanese men married ''picture brides'' from the homeland who later joined them on the sugar plantations.

With the plantation playing a central role in the life of Hawaii, other immigrants joined the Japanese in supporting ''King Sugar''. The Portuguese of Madeira and the Azores sailed for the Hawaiian Islands between 1884-86 after a blight had destroyed their vineyards. Serving as plantation *luna,* or overseers, the Portuguese often cut an imposing figure on their large white horses, wearing knee-high boots and broad-rimmed white Panama hats. In their ''Portuguese camps'' they became known in the islands for their delicious *pao duce* or sweetbreads baked in their distinctive brick ovens.

By the second decade of the twentieth century, the Japanese began to leave the plantations for employment in the towns or independent farming. To support the needs of sugar and pineapple, the planters turned to another source of labor immigration, the Philippines. The first Filipinos had come to the Hawaiian Islands as laborers in 1906 and by the 1930's they were the major labor source for the sugar industry on the Big Island. Laborers from Samoa, Okinawa, Korea and Puerto Rico were also recruited in smaller numbers for plantation labor, transforming all the islands into its modern polyglot of cultures, foods, customs, festivals and lifestyles.

The world of Big Island plantations was a subtle blend of cultural diversity as well as racial separation. Laborers were for the sake of cultural differences kept in their distinct camps designated by ethnic derivations such as "Spanish Camp" or "Japanese Camp." Workers of different nationality were paid different wages to induce jealousies and the distinct, immaculate homes of the managers were, as can be seen in the Puna district, always sitting high on a hill looking down on the laborers. It was just the way of life in an older Hawaii.

But the children of the natives and immigrants eventually changed all this, for they did not feel the restrictions of race and class accepted by their parents. They formed lasting bonds in the island lifestyle that they shared in playground games, diet, dress, attitudes and language. Their parents had spoken the native tongue plus "pidgin" English. The children embraced this island dialect as their first and primary tongue which created a "local identity" more important than race. At home they watched their parents work hard for success and learned to respect family, neighbors and community. In the American schools, they were also taught the values of equal opportunity, freedom and the courage to change inequalities.

During World War II and the post war years these children of the plantation became a major force in small businesses and the new visitor industry, which was opening up exciting new opportunities of advancement. As the sugar plantations waned, modern Hawaii was born in the dreams and aspiration of the plantation children who combined their parents devotion to hard work and success with their American ideals of racial equality. Intermarriage also began to blur traditional racial lines as a new generation of mixed heritage was being born. Of the hundred thousand residents of the Big Island forty per cent of them are of mixed ancestry. Marriages between races have been increasing even among those groups such as the Japanese, who in the past had low intermarriage rates. Today, the fastest growing ethnic group is the part-Hawaiian, an indication that the fears of King Kalakaua have at last been allayed.

The Big Island explorer finds this diversity of the Island people most evident in the community celebrations that comprise the "local style." All races seem represented, especially in the food. The *kalua* or baked pig is brought out of the steaming *imu* beneath the layer of hot rocks and smoldering flavored *kiawe* wood. From inside the pig the hot rocks encased in *ti* leaves are removed, as are the deliciously baked sweet potatoes, breadfruit, *taro* and fish. Added to the evening feast are other traditional island favorites including chicken and octopus *luau* made from *taro* leaves and coconut milk, *teriyaki* chicken and *sushi* and chicken *adobo,* a favored Filipino dish. A Korean specialty, *Kim chee,* fermented Kohala-grown cabbage, spices the meal that includes *chow mein* noodles. For dessert Okinawan donuts and Portuguese *malasada* or sweet fried dough, may be enjoyed. And gallons of American soda and beer will no doubt wash down this *pot pourri* of international cuisine.

Long into the evening the Island people will "talk story" as laughter is intermingled with impromptu Hawaiian songs. At first the music is raucous and the dancing teasing and suggestive. By midnight the tunes are more romantic and sadder. A few of the later partiers, children in tow, are now straggling home guided by the plethora of stars that light Hawaii's sky. A mother lifts her sleeping child from the couch where he has made a temporary nest and returns him to his bed. Her large, brown hands place a blanket over him and then tenderly wipe the hair from his brow. The lights are quietly extinguished.

Sunrise on Hawaii will begin forth another day for the Island people who write their history in their labor, love and song.

These Japanese coffee farmers are but a few of the laborers from Japan who left the sugar plantations to develop Hawaii's coffee industry.
☐Photo: Baron Goto/Bishop Museum

Gathered in front of Hilo's Hawaii Drug Company (circa 1905-1915), these employers and employees represent the multi-cultural nature of turn-of-the-century Hawaii.   ☐Photo: Chock Chong/Bishop Museum

The famous, musical Beamer family of Hawaii representing three generations pose in front of "Hale Huki," their traditional home. From left to right are Isabella Kalili Desha, Baby Beamer (Mrs. Elizabeth Dahlberg) and Helen Desha Beamer.
□Photo: Baker-Van Dyke Collection

Iolani Luahine stands out in modern Hawaii as one of the most excellent dancers of the hula to have performed for contemporary audiences.
☐Photo: Frances Haar

Hula Kahiko – The Dance of the Ancients

Born as Harriet Lanihau Makekau in the village of Napoopoo, as an infant she was hanai or adopted by her great aunt, Keahi Luahine, who had been a dancer in the court of King Kalakaua. At the age of four, the young girl was dedicated to Laka, the goddess of hula, and was given the name Iolani Luahine by her aunt. Skilled in the hula kahiko, the dance of the ancients, in 1940 at the age of twenty-five, she performed in Washington, D.C. at the National Ford Festival of Dance. After the death of her aunt, she perfected her chants and style under the tutelage of the incomparable Mary Kawena

Pukui. Her intense, inspired movements and hypnotic eyes left those who watched her dance with the distinct feeling that they had traversed time, place and culture.

When Iolani Luahine died in 1978, the islands were deprived of one of the true devotees of Laka. "When Iolani dances," as one admiring reviewer wrote, "you feel thousands of years of dancing ancestors concentrated in this one body...dancing for her gods and they through her."

The *paniola* of Hawaii are represented by many races and backgrounds, typified in this historic photograph of Japanese ranch workers. K. Fukushima, standing, was a cowboy for Sam Parker.
☐ Photo: Bishop Museum

Kamehameha Day is a day of Hawaiian pride throughout Hawaii.

The graceful beauty of an island woman is captured at Puuhonua O Honaunau. ☐Photo: Greg Vaughn

A Kupuna (elder) dances to the music of a local hula festival. ☐Photo: Peter French

A *halau* also shows respect for the legendary Pele who makes her home in Kilauea Crater.   □Photo: Greg Vaughn

Four island youngsters pose with their "skimboards" at the seawall in Kona.   □Photo: Bob Fewell

Hawaiian *paniola* exhibit their skills at a Waimea roundup.
☐Photo: Greg Vaughn

Big Island Councilman Kalani Shutte photographed on his horse at his Waimea ranch.
☐Photo: Nobu Nakayama

A group of Big Island friends spend their afternoon motorcycling about the island.
☐Photo: Bob Fewell

Leaping into the ocean (above) or paddling an outrigger canoe (below) are ancient Hawaiian past-times enjoyed in modern Hawaii.   □Photo: Bob Fewell

Pa'u rider Ben Heloca participates in the Kamehameha Day Parade in Kailua- Kona. ☐Photo: Greg Vaughn

Lei makers string lovely tropical flowers into dazzling leis. ☐Photo: Peter French

Guitars and island people are often inseparable. ☐Photo: Greg Vaughn

Andrew Aikau is selected to wear the helmet of an *alii* during Establishment Day Festival at Puukohola Heiau.
☐Photo: Greg Vaughn

The children of Hawaii celebrate May Day with flowers, song and *lei*. ☐Photo: Greg Vaughn

In their simple, innocent beauty, often adorned with plumeria or other flower *lei*, children such as Leialoha Elisaga (above) or the young girls below, are the rising generation of Hawaii's multi-ethnic people. ☐Photo: Greg Vaughn

A young *lei* maker shows off her wreath of plumeria. ☐Photo: Bob Fewell

An island of many nations comes to life in the children of Hawaii.   □Photo: Greg Vaughn

May Day in Hawaii is Lei Day as children at Honaunau School join with schools throughout the state to enjoy special musical festivities.
□Photo: Greg Vaughn

Grandparents take pleasure in the May Day school program at Honaunau.   □Photo: Greg Vaughn

The Tigers baseball team of Honaunau proudly pose with their trophies after a winning season.   □Photo: Greg Vaughn

A Filipino Big Islander shows off his prize fighting chicken used in what has become a controversial though popular ethnic activity. ☐Photo: John E. Bowen

"Auntie Lei" Collins is the former curator at the Daughters of Hawaii's Hulihee Palace. ☐Photo: Greg Vaughn

The social life, gossip and "talk story" of island living are often concentrated in such places as the local barbershop. ☐Photo: Noel Black

Kings, Cowboys and Gods:
North Kohala and Waimea

Waimea's gentle, rolling pasture lands offer a striking contrast to the tropical valleys, volcanic deserts and ocean-swept coastlines of the Big Island. □Photo: Peter French

CHAPTER V

Kings, Cowboys and Gods: North Kohala and Waimea

The greatest Hawaiian King of all was born near the rugged coasts of this haunted land. On a stormy night long before western calendars marked such dates, Kamehameha had been born as a fiery, soaring star signaled his special destiny. In this district of North Kohala he was raised in secrecy and learned not only the arts of war and leadership, but reverence towards his protective gods. Southeastward, the cool, green rolling hills of Waimea also retain the spirit of their historic past. The faded presences of the old-time cattle barons stride boldly across the ranching empires they founded. The rough-and-tumble "Waimea crowd" of white men who came as vagabonds and beachcombers also survive. Just as Kamehameha gave North Kohala the aura of royal greatness, the "wild and wooly" manners of the *paniola* or cowboys gave the highlands of Waimea a distinct, if rustic reputation.

Gentler spirits also pervade the northern landscape. At Kohala, the gods of old Hawaii are still respected at Mookini Heiau and the village of Lapakahi near Mahukona. Reverend Elias Bond's Kalaihiola Church in Hawi and Father Lorenzo Lyon's Imiola Church in Waimea are filled yet with the Hawaiian religious hymns sung joyously for over one hundred years.

The districts of North Kohala and Waimea are indeed haunted by these kings, cowboys and gods of Hawaii. These are lands characterized by small villages, pasture lands, ranches, cool breezes, moist rains and history. In Kamehameha's country, this great chief's birthsite, the ancient temples within which he worshipped, the fields he irrigated with incredible underground tunnels and the isolated Pololu Valley where he was reared, are waiting to be rediscovered. In Kapaau, the Kamehameha Statue is a reminder that this quiet land was once the home of Hawaii's great leader, who in the first decades of the nineteenth century finally unified the separate island districts into a Hawaiian kingdom.

Kamehameha the Great is also credited with giving birth to Waimea as cowboy country. The cool, lush, and green region of Waimea was an ideal region for the first cattle introduced to Hawaii. It was British Captain George Vancouver who offered the monarch a gift of bedraggled longhorns he had taken on at Monterey, California. In 1803, another new creature was introduced to the Hawaiian people when Captain Cleveland of the *Lelia Bird* presented Kamehameha with the gift of several horses. While riding horses became a favorite sport of Hawaiians, the longhorn cattle posed a problem to Kamehameha. Because the King had originally put a *kapu*, or

law, on the animals prohibiting anyone from killing them, the tough breed quickly flourished and was soon running wild.

Then a daring Boston entrepreneur and seaman by the name of John Palmer Parker struck a bargain with Kamehameha that would alter the face of Waimea. The burly, mutton-chopped Parker was a carpenter, blacksmith, cowpoke and jack-of-all-trades who after his arrival in the islands befriended Kamehameha. In 1815, the King hired Parker to domesticate the wild cattle and the young man rose brilliantly to the charge of managing the king's herds. He soon started a herd of his own and then married into the royal family. Thus was born from a vast grassland of 220,000 acres with wild cattle, the century-old dynasty of the Parker Ranch.

Under the guidance of his descendents, especially Colonel Samuel Parker, the massive grazing lands were eventually purchased and consolidated under family control. The cow village thus acquired a new name Kamuela or Samuel in Hawaiian. But a successful ranch needs cowhands and Native Hawaiians had no ranching experience. With the support of Kamehameha III, Spanish and Mexican range riders were hired to train the Hawaiians. These *espanol* or as Hawaiians called them, *paniola*, were expert cowhands who imparted their vast ranching knowledge to the quick-learning natives. By the late nineteenth century, the Hawaiian *paniola* or cowboy was indistinguishable from his wild west counterpart save for the deep brown skin and the lei of fresh flowers adorning his wide-brimmed hat.

The rough and tumble nature of the Waimea cowtown in the nineteenth century was softened somewhat by the establishment in the 1830's of a Protestant missionary station. Desirous to locate a site where exhausted missionary families could find solace and relaxation, Waimea was selected for its verdant countryside, cool springs and refreshing breezes. In charge of the Waimea station was Reverend Lorenzo Lyons who served there as minister for nearly half a century. A gifted poet, his many musical compositions and hymns such as island favorite *Hawaii Aloha* are still popular today.

Modern day Waimea still feels the strong presence of its cowboy past. In addition to Parker Ranch, which runs about fifty thousand head of cattle on land that makes up over five percent of the area on the Big Island, there are more than three hundred and forty ranches on the island, some using the latest in husbandry technology. At Kahua Ranch in Waimea, the age of the electronic cowboy has arrived. At this 22,000-acre spread which extends from the sodden summit of the Kohala Mountains to the bone-dry seacoast, *paniola* mount a "Japanese quarter horse," or motorcycle for a roundup. Three windmills and two commercial wind farms produce approximately three and one half megawatts of electricity. Three computers and a sophisticated communication system connect the owners to their far-flung acreage.

Modern methods of ranching and a new shopping mall do not seem, however, to disturb the spirits of Waimea's past. The northwest country continues to be special because it cannot erase those natural and cultural elements that gave it birth. The kings, cattle barons, native *paniola*, adventurers and missionaries just loom too large.

The Parker Ranch home of owner Richard Smart offers an excellent collection of privately owned art treasures. Recently opened for public viewing, the Parker Ranch grounds, historic structures and art museum provide Waimea visitors with a rare insight into the ranching heritage of Hawaii.
☐Photo: Peter French

On the fog-covered road to "Mana," the historic Parker homestead in Waimea, the traveller is often greeted by cool upland air and a mysterious mist.
☐ Photo: Peter French

A waterfall along the Kohakohau Stream cuts through the valleys of Kohala Mountain. ☐Photo: Greg Vaughn

Horses are an integral part of life in North Kohala. Here a magnificent steed runs free in the green meadows of the Kohala Ranch, easily identified by its miles of distinctive white fencing. □Photo: Dana Edwards

The ever-present Mauna Kea looms above the
cowboy country of Waimea. □Photo: Peter French

The Parker Ranch *paniola* or Hawaiian cowboys seem far more familiar to the western plains of the United States than the tropic lands of the Pacific. □Photo: Greg Vaughn

The history of Waimea is told in great part through the story of the Parker Ranch, commonly called "the largest privately owned ranch in the United States." From its founder John Palmer Parker through the several generations to the present owner, Richard Smart, the Parker Ranch has provided employment, recreation and cultural influences to the people of this upland region. In the early twentieth century, the social life of the community was frequently set by the Parkers who yearly provided Waimea with a large *luau* where enormous amounts of pig, beef, *poi*, fresh fish and other island favorites were prepared and consumed. Matriarch Thelma Parker left behind generous donations for the welfare of the district, memorialized today in the Thelma Parker Library.

Other important names in the history of Waimea ranching have been the Richards and Von Holt families. Since 1928, these families have run the largest herds of Avignon Charolais and commercial Angus cattle in the state. Using artificial insemination methods to improve the strains of their cattle, for twenty years they have successfully cross-bred Brangus, Shorthorn, Simental and Charolais stock.

Ranching has also left its mark on Waimea in the lifestyle of its residents. In their clothing, Texas-style hats, preference for Hawaiian country music and distinct, bowlegged gait, the old-timers illustrate that the influence of cattle reaches well beyond the presence of powerful family ranches. Being a Hawaiian cowboy, quite simply, is a proud distinction of a small but fascinating tradition.

The Hawaiian cowboy can compete with any Texas cowboy in the skill of roping a calf as demonstrated here on the Parker Ranch. ☐Photo: Greg Vaughn

A lifetime of riding the Waimea range gives this *paniola* the tough, weather-beaten pride of a man who knows how to handle his horse, gear and cattle. □Photo: Peter French

The Hawaiian *paniola* came from all backgrounds, for a man was judged by his abilities, not his race.   □Photo: Peter French

Rodeos

The first ''rodeo'' was probably initiated by the Mexican *vaqueros* who were imported to Hawaii to train Native Hawaiians in the arts of ranching. These Espanol, called *paniola* by natives, taught the skills of roping, branding, driving and breeding cattle. Hawaiians excelled at horseback riding and thoroughly enjoyed the life of the open range, learning to track down and lasso wild cattle. On a journey through Waimea country in 1830, Kamehameha III, still a teenager, excitedly showed the Hawaiian love for ranching by impulsively chasing down a wild bullock by himself, successfully lassoing the animal.

Frequent competitors in rodeos in the American West, the Hawaiian *paniola* has consistently won outstanding honors since the last century. Rodeos are still popular in Waimea where several are staged each summer. One of the Hawaiian style competitions is called the ''Poo-Y-U,'' recalling the days when John Palmer Parker and his few, first cowboys caught wild cattle without any help. Lassoing the animal, they would run their rope around a forked tree, loop it through the ''y'' in the tree and then drag the animal up against the tree. In these modern competitions, the spirit of the Old West is given a distinctive Pacific twist.

The patriarchs and matriarchs, including Elizabeth Dowsett Parker (far right) whose grandson, Richard Smart, is the present-day owner of Parker Ranch, pose for their portrait on the lanai of their homestead. ☐Photo: Prince Kuhio/Baker-Van Dyke Collection

Hawaiian cowboys branding cattle in old Waimea, as depicted in this photograph, is reminiscent of similar scenes in the American West.
☐Photo: Baker-Van Dyke Collection

Eben Low, legendary paniolo of Waimea at far right and his brother-in-law James Hind (left) relax with an unidentified friend at the ranch at Kiholo, having just returned from hunting wild turkeys. ☐Photo: Prince Kuhio/Baker-Van Dyke Collection

The North Kohala Coast, as viewed from Kohala Mountain towards Mauna Kea, is a land of royal births, legendary heroes and the persistent winds of good fortune. ☐ Photo: Greg Vaughn

Riding off into the sunset at Waikiʻi Ranch, located high on the slopes of Mauna Kea in the heart of the Parker Ranch.
□Photo: Waikiʻi Ranch

Polo has had a long, aristocratic tradition in Hawaii as a sport of the upper-crust *kamaaina* or long-time residents. □ Photo: Greg Vaughn

The women of the Hawaiian Civic Club prepare strings of *lei* in preparation for the festivities of Kamehameha Day.
□Photo: Peter French

The statue of King Kamehameha the Great in Kohala is adorned with *lei* for Kamehameha Day. □Photo: Peter French

A story is frequently told in Hawaii about the King Kamehameha Statue, the famous warrior King's monument in Honolulu that has been photographed and admired by millions. When the Hawaiian Kingdom commissioned an Italian artist to complete the statue in the late 1870's, many people of the Kohala district requested that the statue be placed near the Monarch's birthplace in their home district. After all, it seemed most fitting that the statue of Kamehameha grace the land of his birth and greatest pleasures. Of course, the statue had been designated for Honolulu where it would serve most effectively as a symbol of national pride. The

request was denied, even though the more insightful predicted that the statue would never reach Honolulu.

The ship carrying the completed statue to Hawaii sank off the Falkland Islands as it approached Cape Horn and the King Kamehameha statue was lost. A second statue was ordered, which was successfully completed and erected in Honolulu in time for the coronation of King Kalakaua in 1882. The fate of the first statue? It was salvaged a few years later, its broken extended arm repaired and sold to the Hawaiian government. It can be seen today where it had been prophesied to stand–in Kohala.

The picturesque country of Waimea is dramatically
framed in the snarled limbs of upland trees.
Photo: Lee Allen Thomas

Keokea Beach Park in North Kohala consists of seven, sloping acres bordering a rocky, imposing coastline. ☐ Photo: Greg Vaughn

***Poi* pounders are just a few of the artifacts** of ancient Hawaiian civilization to be explored at Lapakahi State Historical Park, the site of a several-hundred-year-old fishing village. A remarkable experience in "living history," a stroll through Lapakahi village vividly reveals how *ka poe kahiko*, the people of old, lived, worked, fished, played and prayed in a time now lost forever.
□Photo: Greg Vaughn

Mookini Heiau is a sacred vestige of the complex religion which once thrived on Hawaii. The unusually high walls, tradition says, were constructed in the sixteenth century by the legendary *kahuna* Paao. In a single night, thousands of basalt stones were transported to the site hand-to-hand by a human chain from Pololu Valley which is several miles to the north. The *kahu* or caretaker of the present day *heiau* is Momi Lum, the latest in a long line of Mookini descendants who have been entrusted with the care of the temple.   □Photo: Peter French

Legends

When Reverend William Ellis travelled through North Kohala in 1823, he heard from the people several remarkable legends, some of which spoke of foreign visitors long before the arrival of Captain Cook. Hawaiians told Ellis that hundreds of years before a white *kahuna* or priest came to this part of Hawaii, bringing with him two idols, one large and the other small. These gods were adopted by the people and the temple of Mookini built for them at the direction of the white priest, who was called Paao. They also spoke of Kana, a Kohala warrior so tall that he could walk through the sea from one island to another or straddle the islands of Oahu and Kauai. He was also credited with having travelled to Tahiti to recapture the sun which had been stolen by natives from that place.

Another legend involved the adventures of Kamapiikai, a priest of a Kohala temple. In a vision, Kamapiikai had been shown the mythical land of Tahiti to which he travelled with his companions. Fifteen years later he returned speaking of a land called Haupokane where not only there was abundant life and beauty, but a mysterious stream of enduring long life. No matter how ill, tired or infirm, bathing in the stream restored one's health, strength and youth. Kamapiikai made four journeys to Haupokane, the natives explained to the missionary. He never returned from the last trip, and the place of eternal life was lost.

Waimanu Valley stretches out towards the ocean, her land covered in rich foliage along the Hamakua Coast.
☐Photo: Greg Vaughn

Where Sugar was King:
Waipio Valley and The Hamakua Coast

CHAPTER VII

Where Sugar was King: Waipio Valley and The Hamakua Coast

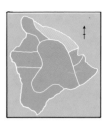

When viewed from the ocean or air, the northeast districts of the island of Hawaii do not look like they once were inhabited by large native villages and later, teeming sugar industries. As one peers down from the steep cliffs of Waipio into the valley, it seems unlikely that thousands of Hawaiians once cultivated *taro* in her basin, fished in her waters or rode the powerful surf to her shores. The secluded, lonely land echoes the words of an old Hawaiian man, who in the late nineteenth century told visitor Isabella Bird that "he's very unhappy; he says, soon there will be no more Kanakas." The legendary home of Hawaiian kings and gods was being reclaimed by the persistent tropical vines and ferns.

A tranquil nature is also reclaiming the Hamakua Coast with its dramatic series of rugged, deep-cut ravines and cascading waterfalls that carry the melted snows of Mauna Kea back to the sea. The highland is green with the lush sugar cane that seems to grow from every inch of accessible land, from the steep ocean cliffs *mauka* to the slopes of Mauna Kea. The tall, white chimneys of the sugar mills rise dramatically from this otherwise picturesque haven of nature; a reminder of a time when railroads, mule-drawn trucks and thousands of immigrant laborers busily traversed the landscape, planting, irrigating, cutting, burning, loading and hauling sugar cane.

Sugar was once King in Hawaii, and the land, people and lifestyles vibrated in unison with the desire for sweet gold. Enjoying the rich, flowing waters of Mauna Kea and a luxurious rainfall, the forty miles of northern coast from Hilo to Honokaa was well-suited for the plantation crop that consumed tons of water per acre. In wetland Hamakua where sugar could flourish, an industry responded by converting every acre of usable land into the growing of cane.

The laborers came from China, Japan, Portugal and the Philippines and they settled in plantation camps that had once been native villages called Onomea, Papaaloa, Papaikou, Honomu, Laupahoehoe and Honohina. Their wages were meager, the work relentless and dreary, but families and communities flourished. At Laupahoehoe, for example, nestled along the coastline of Hamakua, a hotel, stores, a post office, churches, Buddhist temples and a jail complete with a native sheriff comprised a bustling village. When the plantations improved transportation over the steep ravines by building a modern railroad in the early twentieth century, a vital link to supplies, information and visitors further transformed what had once been sleepy native villages into frontier towns.

Men, women and even children worked on those early sugar plantations. Since sugar grew in a two year cycle, there was always a routine of labor to be performed. These unending tasks included *hana hoe* or weeding which was often performed by children, *hanawai*, irrigation, *kutch ken*, cutting cane or *hapai ko*, loading the cane on trucks, or railroad cars. The fields were literally blanketed with workers wielding hoes or cane knives or hoisting large bundles of cane across their shoulders.

The air of Hamakua was often filled during the harvest season with the acrid black smoke of burning cane. The fields had been torched to burn off the chaff and destroy the centipedes and rats that infested the fields. The burnt, exposed cane would then be cut and hauled to the sugar mills where it was processed into molasses or unrefined sugar.

At Haina Landing below Honokaa, large transport ships would then be filled with the molasses, which was pumped through large hoses to the ships' tanks. A diver would connect the hose to the ship as crowds from the cliffs above cheered the daring worker. Large, empty barrels tied to the hoses bobbed in the ocean for several days as the slow-pouring molasses was finally loaded on the ships.

Life along the Hamakua Coast did not always mean work. On Saturday nights the Portuguese families would pull back the chairs in their parlors, bring out their mandolins and ukuleles and dance and sing well into the early morning. Travelling troupes of Filipino performers would visit remote plantation camps and entertain the men with the love songs and dances of the homeland. And late night gatherings were often the scene of ghostlore, as the Hamakua Coast was rich with the stories of ancient ghostly night marchers and the mystical *menehune* who played tricks on the late night traveller.

At the busy town of Honokaa with its western-style falsefront stores and buildings, plantation children purchased Chinese sweet-sour plum, Japanese rice crackers or shave ice. By the 1930's a movie theater was showing American and Japanese films. Especially unforgettable was the excitement when flying banners would announce a new Japanese silent movie to be shown with *benshi* narration. The *benshi* was a narrator who told the story of the movie while impersonating all the male and female character voices. Whatever their race, adults and youngsters in the plantation camps thrilled at the *samurai* and terrifying Japanese *obake* or ghost classics given life by the narrator.

Sugar remains an important crop in Hamakua, but it no longer commands the landscape. Like the *taro* and rice farms in Waipio, the once bustling plantation camps of Hamakua have become quiet. Sugar cane trucks still haul down the coast to Hilo and the black cane fire smoke still darkens the sky, but the pace of life has become slower and older. Nature's power is resilient and as human activity ebbs, she extends her calm over the land sugar once ruled.

The steep, inaccessible cliffs north of Waipio Valley are a rugged barrier to further travel on land. ☐Photo: Peter French

Taro cultivation is an ancient Hawaiian agricultural skill still maintained in remote Waipio Valley.
☐ Photo: Greg Vaughn

A mule train loaded with taro winds up the steep road out of Waipio Valley in this 1936 photograph.
☐Photo: Baker-Van Dyke Collection

The interior of Waipio Valley in 1886 was far more populated with Hawaiian and Chinese farmers, dwelling
houses, stores and churches, than it is today.   ☐Photo: Albert Lyons/Baker-Van Dyke Collection

In 1933, when ''King Sugar'' ruled the Hamakua Coast, plantations such as Papaaloa Mill were the territories most powerful and important industries. Note the arrow and mileage to Hilo painted on the roof of the mill for the purposes of directing the island's early airplanes. ☐Photo: Baker-Van Dyke Collection

Laupahoehoe was an important settlement in 1880 partly because of the frequency of loading passengers and cargo to awaiting offshore ships. In 1946 a tidal wave washed over Laupahoehoe Point, killing several school children and marking the decline of the community as a population center. ☐Photo: J.A.Gonsalves/Baker-Van Dyke Collection

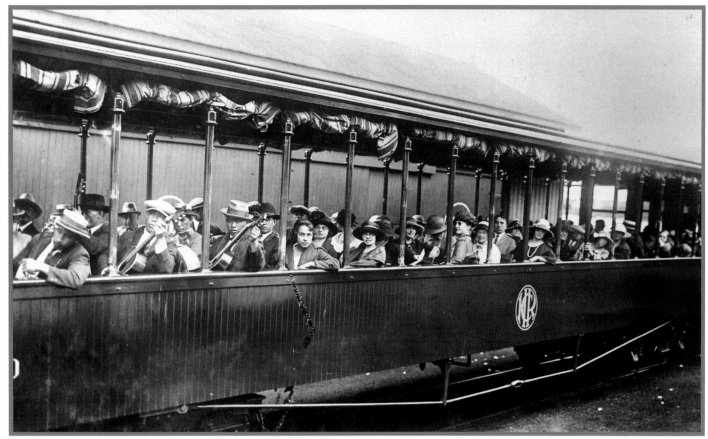

The Hilo Consolidated Railway carried passengers across the once difficult-to-traverse Hamakua Coast. In this 1926 photograph, visitors in the passenger car are being serenaded by a Hawaiian orchestra from the inter-island-sland steamer, *S. S. Haleakala*.
☐Photo: Tai Sing Loo/ Baker-Van Dyke Collection

The train pulls out of the station along the Hamakua Coast.
☐Photo:Baker-Van Dyke Collection

The town of Honomu reflects the multi-cultural influences that shaped plantation society, from the western-style, false-front stores to Chinese markets, Hawaiian Christian Churches and Japanese Buddhist temples with their distinct architecture. ☐Photo: Peter French

Hakalau Mill is hand-tinted in this early photograph when sugar was the undisputed "King" of Hawaii. □Photo: Bishop Museum

Sugar Towns

The decline of the sugar plantation as a major economic force in Hawaii has shrunk the populations of the Hamakua Coast, which once teemed with thousands of laborers. A journey through the little plantation towns of Honokaa, Paauilo, Papaaloa, Honomu, Papaikou or Pepeekeo reveal an older population, men and women who are retired from the sugar industry yet who still live on this coast they once helped to cultivate and develop into a major industry. Their memories are keen as they remember their youths on the Hamakua Coast, growing up in immigrant camps, working as children for a nickel a day in the long rows of sugar cane while attending American and foreign language schools. Here on the Hamakua Coast they matured, married and raised their own families and then watched their communities quietly fade. When they come of age, the young people want to move out for the opportunities elsewhere, while the elders share their yesteryears in the recreational centers, barbershops and storefront benches that have been the traditional settings for "talk story."

Not that the Hamakua Coast has given up. Sugar is still being planted and efforts at diversified agriculture has witnessed the dramatic growth of macadamia orchards in Honokaa. The scenic drive to Laupahoehoe attracts an increasing number of visitors and the Hawaii Tropical Botanical Garden just north of Hilo offers a luxurious variety of native and foreign flora. With the spirit of risk that was so much a part of its past, Hamakua's history is still being written.

Sugar cane tassels glint in the sunlight as the young cane plants grow in the warm Hawaiian sun.
□Photo: Peter French

Leaves of the maturing sugar cane sway in the almost constant trade winds that blow across the Hamakua coast.
☐Photo: Nobu Nakayama

The Hamakua Coast's rugged ravines and steep seacliffs gradually become smaller as they near Hilo Bay.
☐Photo: Nobu Nakayama

Looking down the Hamakua Coast towards Hilo.
□Photo: Peter French

A Pacific Town: Hilo

The Pacific town of Hilo awakens as sunrise illuminates
distant Mauna Kea with a pink glow.
☐ Photo: Charles Jeffrey

CHAPTER VIII

A Pacific Town: Hilo

A visit to the Pacific town of Hilo in the Victorian age usually required an uncomfortable inter-island passage across the rough channel waters between Maui and Hawaii. Crowded into shabby steamers such as the *Kilauea,* passengers joined Englishmen, Chinese merchants, native Hawaiians and Americans who were crowded on the decks or leaning precariously over the rails. Cargo, trunks and portmanteaus were packed in every available space and, the saloon was heaped with Mexican saddles and saddlebags, an indispensable item for travel on the Big Island.

As the steamer approached Hilo Bay, canoes filled with natives would come off the shore, followed by husky swimmers and surf-board riders. A crowd of natives bedecked in leis and floral hats could be seen forming on the landing. All of Hilo town seemed to be moving towards the bay, *pa'u* or skirted lady riders raced through the dusty village bridle paths to the place where the *Kilauea* passengers were to land. A whale-boat, manned by "eight young men in white linen suits and white straw hats with wreaths of carmine-colored flowers round both hats and throats," rowed out to greet the passengers. They were singing gleefully as other natives of Hilo came on board, extending *aloha, lei,* handshakes and hugs.

Hilo in those days was a beautiful, verdant town that spoke well for its tropical setting. "What Honolulu attempts to be," adventuress Isabella Bird noted, "Hilo is without effort." The town presented to her a bewildering maze of lilies, roses, fuchsias, clematis, begonias, convolvuli, the huge granadilla, the purple and yellow water lemons, also varieties of custard apples, rose apples, mangoes, mangostein guavas, bamboos, alligator pears, oranges, tamarinds, papayas, bananas, breadfruit, magnolias, geraniums, candle-nut, gardenias, dracaenas, eucalyptus, pandanus and quantities of other trees and flowers.

Hilo is still a Pacific town of floral colors, tropic architecture and hospitable island people, all nestled dramatically at the base of majestic Mauna Kea and Mauna Loa. While the speed and comfort of passage to Hawaii has vastly improved, Hilo has retained the characteristic charm and relaxed atmosphere that caused Miss Bird to proclaim its superiority to other Hawaiian towns. Despite the challenges of tidal waves and approaching lava flows, through war, development and growth, Hilo remains a town of history and natural beauty.

Her history is found in her rejuvenated downtown square where turn-of-the-century buildings are finding a renewed life as restaurants and shops.

The attentive eye discerns fascinating nuggets of Hawaii's past; in front of the state library is the *pinao* stone, which once graced a native Hawaiian temple and the legendary *naha* stone. It is said that Kamehameha as a young man proved his destiny to rule the islands by lifting the five thousand pound *naha*. In the downtown park, a sundial donated to Hilo by King Kalakaua, the "Merry Monarch," still marks the passage of time.

The religious heritage of Hilo is represented in the apricot colored, wooden Haili Church built in 1859 through the efforts of Christian Hawaiians and American Protestant missionaries. Nearby is the oldest house remaining in Hilo, the home of missionaries Reverend David Belden Lyman and his wife, Sarah Joiner Lyman. Built in 1839 as a home for the Lymans and their eight children, the distinctive New England-style house was a center in the last century for education, medical assistance, Hilo's social life and the establishment of the Hilo Boy's Boarding School.

The natural beauty of Hilo is relished in her spacious and well-kept private lawns and landscapes, and in the public parks, gardens, beaches and coastline that offer unique settings and sights. At Rainbow Falls the Wailuku River dramatically cascades into a deep-water pond enjoyed for its cool bathing. Fifteen miles to the north is Akaka Falls State Park where the four hundred foot Kahuna Falls and the four hundred and twenty foot Akaka Falls are visible from a path that leads through a lush tropical garden and bamboo forest. The thirty-acre park located at the southern end of Hilo Bay is Liliuokalani Gardens, a traditional Japanese garden ideal for meditation or viewing the tranquil waters of Hilo Bay. Nani Mau Gardens, "forever beautiful," is a twenty-acre orchard that nurtures more than one hundred kinds of tropical fruit trees combined with orchids, ginger and anthuriums.

But the real Hilo is best discovered wherever her people congregate to shop, work, sing, dance or play. Hilo is a fascinating town of small shops where artisans create Hawaiian bowls or weave *lauhala* hats; where merchants sell Japanese merchandise or Chinese salted plum candies; where main street America takes on a Polynesian or Asian character. Hilo is Suisan Fish Market at sunrise when the fishing boats auction their tons of colorful, lively catch to restaurateurs and fishmongers. The spirit of Hilo finds expression in the many Christian and Buddhist churches and festivals where the several generations of island people join in prayer, song and sometimes dance.

The greatest dance festival throughout the Hawaiian Islands also takes place in Hilo once a year. Dozens of *hula halau* or Hawaiian *hula* schools throughout the islands and mainland convene in Hilo to engage in two magnificent days of Hawaiian dance and celebration. Named for King David Kalakaua who helped to revive a pride and respect for the once disdained native *hula*, the Merrie Monarch Festival has become one of the world's greatest dance competitions.

If the Victorian visitors of yesterday could return to present-day Hilo, they would see a great many changes. Urban streets, subdivisions, modern buildings and traffic have reshaped the turn-of-the-century Pacific town. Yet, in the tempo of life and hospitality, in the easy blend of nature and structure, they perhaps could still recognize old Hilo. A town's identity, like that of a human personality, persists through time.

Onomea Falls, at Hawaii Tropical Botanical Garden, gushes through the jungles of the Big Island.
☐ Photo: Greg Vaughn

Sampan cruising into Wailoa River heading for Suisan
Fish Market. □Photo: Peter French

Modern Hilo retains the ambience of an early Pacific town despite the increasing street traffic.
☐ Photo: Peter French

Wailoa State Park in Hilo provides a delightful recreational area for picnics, family outings and quiet retreats.   □Photo: Peter French

The sampans of Hilo bring in their fresh ocean catch to be sold to restaurants, markets, wholesalers and families.   □Photo: Peter French

Sampan Fleet

The Japanese sampan fleet was one of the many contributions that the immigrant from Japan made to the style of fishing in Hawaii. The small, highly maneuverable boat was ideal for navigating island currents and could be handled by fewer men than most other watercraft. Until the tidal waves of 1946 and 1960 reshaped the Hilo waterfront, the sampan fleet would be crowded into Wailoa River and Hilo Bay. Although throwing a fishing net has been seen as a Hawaiian skill, the smaller throw net was also the contribution of Japanese immigrants. Like the sampan, the throw net fishing technique was quickly adapted by other ethnic groups to become one of the many multi-cultural aspects of island life.

A colorful variety of Hawaii's fish, cooled in ice, await purchase during the auctions at Suisan Fish Market.   □Photo: Hugo de Vries

Young workers at Suisan Fish Market display the catch of the day—fresh *tako* or octopus which will soon be sliced and eaten raw as a favorite island delicacy.   □Photo: Cindy Turner

The covered sidewalks of downtown Hilo retain the charm and activity that have long characterized this port town.
☐Photo: Noel Black

Me Kong Grocery in Hilo illustrates the continued infusion of Asian customs and tastes as the foods of Laos, Vietnam, the Philippines and China become popular.
□ Photo: Noel Black

Kamehameha Avenue in downtown Hilo is lined with traffic in anticipation of
the arrival of an inter-island steamer in 1924. □ Photo:Baker-Van Dyke Collection

Hilo waterfront with wooden boat being built on the shore.
□ Photo: Chase/Baker-Van Dyke Collection

Sampans moored alongside dockside houses, 1908.
☐Photo: Baker-Van Dyke Collection

The Japanese tea ceremony is performed with delicate intricacy during Hilo's International Festival. □Photo: Greg Vaughn

Hilo Lifestyle

Each ethnic group that has settled in Hilo has contributed their unique customs, festivities or foods to the life of the community as a whole. Life in Hilo cannot be appreciated without noting the many Oriental, Hawaiian, American and even Creole foods available in stores, restaurants and take-out stands. One of Hilo's own food creations is the local favorite called "locomoco." A hamburger patty and fried egg placed upon a scoop of rice and dowsed in gravy, the "locomoco" was born and bred in Hilo, possibly uniting the American hamburger with the Japanese rice, meat and fried egg dish, *donburi*.

Festivals in Hilo are continuous throughout the year, from Portuguese Catholic celebrations, to Chinese New Years, Japanese *obon* dance festivals, Filipino Rizal Day and an American Christmas on the grounds of the Lyman House Museum.

Sumo wrestlers have long been a part of the Hawaii scene, sumo wrestling being a favorite sport among the early immigrants from Japan.
☐Photo: Greg Vaughn

Chinese "sweet and sour" candies are sold in a small Hilo store to the legions of Hawaii youngsters who devour the uniquely seasoned lemon slices, plums, dried apricots, prunes and other fruits. ☐Photo: Noel Black

The Japanese American population of Hilo has been proud of its heritage, reflected in a growing interest in the art objects of Japan. □Photo: Noel Black

The pride and power of the Hawaiian heritage has in recent years found a new meaning in the celebration of the Merrie Monarch Festival. Both men and women *hula halau* enter the internationally known competition of ancient and modern dancing styles. □Photo: William Waterfall

Merrie Monarch

For the Hawaiian and Hawaiian-at-heart, no festival compares to that of the annual Merrie Monarch Hula Festival during which an available hotel room in crowded Hilo is a great rarity.

The idea for a statewide *hula* competition staged in Hilo originated in 1963 when Hilo residents George Naope and Gene Wilheim suggested the festival as a way to draw international attention to the small Pacific town. By 1971, the competition had grown to a major program with *hula halau* or schools journeying from around the state to dance in a variety of categories including the ancient dance, *hula kahiko* and *hula awana* or modern dance.

The dancers are judged by experienced *hula* teachers on movement, costume, adornments, style, stance and manner.

Staged for several days every April at the Hilo Hoolulu Tennis Stadium, the Merrie Monarch competition is broadcast by television throughout the state. The excited interest that the festival now commands speaks well to the multi-cultural society of Hilo. In the small town where a dozen ethnic groups live together in casual harmony and mutual respect, West, East and the Pacific are vibrant elements in the fabric of day-to-day existence.

The legacy of the Protestant missionary influence is preserved in Hilo's oldest Western house, the home of Reverend David Belden Lyman and Sarah Joiner Lyman.
□Photo: Greg Vaughn

In the pantry of the Lyman House, visitors can view the implements used in the last century in food preparation.
□Photo: Peter French

The Hawaiian quilt was a product of Yankee technique and Hawaiian imagination. The quilt pictured here was designed by Deborah "Kepola" Kakalia and is entitled *Kuu Puai Paoakalani*, Queen Liliuokalani's Flower Garden.
□Photo: Peter French

Every Christmas the Lyman House grounds come alive with a variety of activities, including the *keiki hula* dancers. □Photo: Greg Vaughn

Liliuokalani Gardens, nearby Hilo's famous Banyan Drive, is a Japanese garden with stone sculptures, bridges, tea ceremony house and tranquil walks.
□Photo: Greg Vaughn

Nani Mau Gardens has one of the largest collections of orchids in Hawaii, as well as this brilliant Red Jade Vine. Photo: Douglas Peebles

Rainbow Falls on the Wailuku River.
Photo: Greg Vaughn

A Land that Flames and Blooms: Puna

When the fire of Pele touches the cool waters of Puna, the explosive colors and sounds are indescribable.
☐Photo: Peter French

CHAPTER IX
A Land that Flames and Blooms:
Puna

The land of Puna belongs to Pele. When she desires to bathe, she often rises from her Kilauea home and flows seaward across the districts of Kapoho, Kalapana or Kaimu to rush into the cool waters of the sea. She moves boldly over this land, consuming obstacles in her path with a relentless tide of stone-melting fire. Her enormous power commands respect, for her's is the ability to create the earth. In Puna, she makes the land flame and bloom.

The natural miracle through which lava rock is transformed into verdant flora is being enacted continually on the Big Island. Indeed, in the not too distant geological past, all of Hawaii was an inhospitable desert of cooling, once molten rock. Born from the eruptive activity of Mauna Kea, Mauna Loa, Kilauea, Hualalai and Kohala volcanoes, the island was initially a barren wasteland of smooth *pahoehoe* and rough *aa* lava, where no flora or fauna could exist. (*Pahoehoe* was lava that flowed like molten gold and hardened to a smooth, black surface; *aa* was the clinkery cinder piles with a denser and more porous core.) The erosion of wind, rain and sea eventually produced a thin soil cover which could nurture the seeds carried across the Pacific by the trade winds or birds. Each time a different seed or spore landed and survived and grew, another plant life became established.

Botanists now estimate that four hundred and ten species of plants successful germinated in the Hawaiian islands, an average of one species every 20,000 years dating from the time of the islands creation. Most of these plants probably originated in the Indo-Pacific area to the south and west of Hawaii, although it is estimated that a small percent may have come from the Americas.

Evolving from this stock of 410 species, as many as 1,400 native types of flowering plants would eventually flourish in the Hawaiian islands, many of them specifically adapted to the Hawaiian soil and climate. By including subspecies, varieties and forms, the list of taxonomic floral groups expands to 2,700, of which ninety one percent are endemic to the islands.

In addition to the wind, ocean currents, and birds, early Polynesian settlers also brought to Hawaii additional plants and flowers. Taro, sweet potatoes, *ti* root to manufacture the intoxicant *awa* and sugar cane were carried for the purpose of food. The *kukui* or candlenut tree was also imported for the use of the oil as a lamp fuel. The mulberry tree or *wauke* was brought to Hawaii for use of the bark, which is pounded into *kapa,* a cloth used for bedding and clothing. The ancient Hawaiians also carried some flowering plants. Believing that flowers pleased the gods, they used them to beautify their villages and to adorn themselves at religious events and other celebrations. So treasured were their flowers that their word for them, *pua,* also was used to mean child. For many occasions, the Hawaiians helped convey their feelings by giving or wearing flower *lei* or wreaths, a tradition still practiced.

Later immigrants from East and West brought to the islands more species of vegetables, fruits, trees and flowers. Sub-polar deserts, mountain slopes, lush tropical rain forests, hot arid lava fields, sandy beaches, rocky shorelines and coastal bluffs, each enabled a great variety of newly introduced plants to adapt. Many additional plants were introduced by nineteenth century settlers helping to produce today's lush foliage.

The traveller to Puna is immediately struck not only by the scorching flame of Pele, but by the abundant flora naturally and commercially grown that pleases the eye and scents the air. In the district of Puna, one can discover samples of most of Hawaii's flowering plants, fruits and vegetables. In spring the tops of the giant jacaranda trees are crowned with periwinkle blue clusters of flowers. There are also numerous species of palm trees while bananas grow profusely as do lichee trees, which yield luscious grape-textured fruit encased in shells.

Orchids grow everywhere in Puna, from well-tended home gardens to commercial farms and wild forests. They vary from the small inexpensive ''Miss Joaquim'' vandas, used for food decorations, to the giant cattleya. Another exotic bloom is the blue-green jade vine flower. Native to the rain forests of Luzon, these two-inch-long flowers resemble intricate jade carvings. Anthurium is another well-known Big Island flowering plant found in Puna. From the valentine-like miniatures to huge, red flowers with brilliant yellow spikes, the anthurium is a distinctive plant that adorns homes, festivals and special ceremonies.

In the cooler, higher areas closer to Kilauea crater, there is an abundance of flowers that prefer these more temperate locations. The main flowering tree is the *ohia lehua* whose bright blossoms were sacred to Pele. Picking these blossoms is said to anger Pele, causing her to send down lashings of rain. An even worse sacrilege is the picking of the *ohelo,* a berry sacred to Pele. During eruptions that threaten settled areas, Big Islanders still make special offerings of *ohelo* berries to appease the goddess of fire.

''It was a dream, a rapture, this maze of form and color, this entangled luxuriance, this bewildering beauty,'' wrote Isabella Bird during her tour of the Big Island, ''through which we caught glimpses of a heavenly sky above, while far away, below glade and lawn, shimmered in surpassing loveliness the cool blue of the Pacific.'' In the rare combination of a peaceful floral wilderness, fringed with black sand beaches, azure sky and deep blue seas, Miss Bird perfectly captured the magnificence of this island of flame and bloom. Hawaii overwhelms the senses and weakens the resolve to return to a former, less colorful life. Having once walked her beaches, gazed her vistas and enjoyed her hospitality, the traveller will inevitably return to this realm of beauty, history and fire.

The Black Sand Beach at Kalapana is world famous for its fine, black lava sand and gracious royal palms.
☐ Photo: Peter French

The delectable fruit of the papaya has been enjoyed in Hawaii since the early 1800's when is was imported to the islands from South America. It grows best at low elevations with plenty of sunshine and rain. Puna's papaya is outstandingly tasty.　☐Photo: Nobu Nakayama

The papaya tree has a very distinct shape as can be seen in this close-up of the crowns.　☐Photo: Greg Vaughn

The succulent flesh of the papaya is a real tropical taste treat.
☐Photo: Greg Vaughn

Macadamia orchards are increasingly replacing sugar as the Big Island diversifies its agricultural base.   ☐Photo: Greg Vaughn

Macadamia trees were introduced to Hawaii in 1881 when W. H. Purvis planted some nuts at Honokaa. The trees only became commercially viable when a nut husking machine was developed in 1939.
☐Photo: Greg Vaughn

Ohia lehua flowers were once popular for making leis. These flowers were held to be sacred to Pele, the goddess of the volcano. It was believed that Pele would cause rain to fall on those who picked the blossoms without first making the proper offering.
☐Photo: Greg Vaughn

Heliconia—glorious splashes of floral elegance—are now grown in quantity in Hawaii's muggy, warm lowlands. They dot the humid rain forests of tropical America. ☐Photo: Peter French

Originally from tropical America, anthuriums now even grow wild in some shaded Big Island valleys. The cultivation and hybridization of these almost unreal "plastic" flowers is an important business for Hawaii.
☐Photo: Greg Vaughn

Torch ginger is the most magnificent of the gingers and one of the most spectacular flowers in the world. The plant is made up of large, sparse, cane-like stalks, sometimes twenty feet high. Each stalk holds alternate leaf blades, pointed and up to two feet or more in length. ☐Photo: Peter French

These exquisite, gorgeous and elegant blooms were first carried to the islands by Chinese immigrants. Since then, hundreds of species and hybrids of orchids have emerged. □Photo: Nobu Nakayama

One of the most ubiquitous plants of Hawaii, hibiscus is seen in almost every garden, with numerous hybrids of dazzling color appearing every year. □Photo: Nobu Nakayama

Because the hibiscus flowers possess the unusual trait of not wilting for a day after it is picked, it can be used for many forms of floral decoration. However, since it is easily crushed and bruised and can stain clothes, it is not used for leis. □Photo: Mark Watanabe

Fan palms have recently become popular ornamentals around resorts in Hawaii. Primarily from Asia and Fiji, they add tropical splendor to landscaping. Although not native to Hawaii they recall the days when Hawaii's lowlands and mountains were graced with over forty species of native fan palms. □Photo: Peter French

Globes of frilly, tulip-shaped flowers, resembling lopsided cups of molten steel, protrude boldly from the African tulip tree. □Photo: Peter French

Cymbidium orchids, originally from the East Indies have two to three foot long narrow leaves. The flowers are mainly yellow and pink. ☐ Photo: Greg Vaughn

The night blooming cereus is actually a Mexican cactus brought by a sea captain to present to a missionary teacher. It opens its great buds at about eight o'clock in the evening at periodic intervals between June and October. ☐ Photo: Peter French

The vista of Mountain View and Kurtistown encompasses the Puna district which is becoming a commercial growing center for the Big Island's distinct anthuriums and orchids.
☐ Photo: Peter French

A Hawaiian family greets their friend at Kapoho in 1894.
□Photo: Prince Kuhio/Baker-Van Dyke Collection

As Isabella Bird journeyed through the Puna district, she was captivated by the rich foliage and fruits that grew throughout the area. She was particularly impressed by the breadfruits, rose-crimson apples of the eugenia, the golden guava and the palm tree. ''Here they stood in thousands,'' she wrote of the palms, ''young as well as old, their fronds gigantic, their stems curving every way, and the golden light, which is peculiar to them, toned into a golden green.

The abundance of palm trees, however, symbolized the tragic irony of a land bountiful in tropical vegetation, but devoid of the once plentiful native Hawaiian population. The first censuses of the 1830's reveal the devastating effect of foreign diseases and cultural upheaval on the native race. A land once covered by teeming villages, *taro lo'i* or cultivated terraces, thriving fishponds and the sounds of newborn children, was becoming strangely still. In 1830, 130,000 Hawaiians had survived the first contact with Western civilization. By 1870, 70,000 Hawaiians survived. By the end of the 19th century, only a total of 44,000 Hawaiians existed in the Hawaiian islands.

Miss Bird moved through the expansive terrain of Hawaii, visiting emptied villages where she saw firsthand what many considered to be the passing of the Hawaiian race. She would inquire where all the people had gone, possibly assuming that the villages were deserted by younger Hawaiians moving to the many growing port towns at Hilo, Lahaina or Honolulu. *''Kanaka pau,''* was the melancholy answer given to her inquiry by the few survivors. The people were dead.

A Hawaiian couple poses for their portrait in the Puna district.
☐Photo: Baker-Van Dyke Collection

As the modern traveller follows in the footsteps of historic visitors who explored the largely depopulated lands of Puna, the imagination forces upon itself images of what these old villages must have looked like before they became "haunted by ghosts and horned owls." The *halepili* or grass houses are gone now as well as the unaffected *aloha* that made Hawaiian hospitality world-famous. There are no extensive *taro* farms in the uplands and the ocean is not filled with canoes, frolicking children or men and women fishing. The *heiau* or temples are in ruin, their spiritual power in decline or misunderstood by the *haole* or foreigners of all races, who now inhabit much of the land. The ancient crafts are not being passed on from generation to generation as feather-weaving, woodcarving, *lauhala* matting, *tapa*-making and the hundreds of other advanced skills of the Hawaiian culture remain in the possession of but a few. The dance, music and amusements of the Hawaiian civilization are being revived in modern style, but little opportunity exists in Hawaii to share a bowl of two-finger *poi* and fish with a Hawaiian family who can open the visitor's eyes to the worldview and oral traditions of that once ancient Polynesian race. While the beauty of nature has survived in Hawaii, human culture continues to be as fragile as time and modernity seem to always erode an older, more harmonious way of life.

The traveller presses on through Puna, shutting off those saddening thoughts of a distant past to which only the most privileged few still have access.

The *albrizzia* trees alongside the road near Lava Tree State Park appear as a natural tunnel. ☐Photo: Peter French

An old Puna church was destroyed when a flow of lava consumed it in a hot, barren embrace.
Photo: Peter French

The historic Star of the Sea Church in Kalapana was spared by Pele in her recent eruptions. □Photo: Greg Vaughn

Brilliant religious folk-art graces the ceilings and walls of this famous painted church. ☐Photo: Douglas Peebles

The Queen's Bath was a cold, fresh-water spring in which ancient and contemporary bathers refreshed themselves from the heat of Puna. In the recent eruptions of Puu O'o, Queen's Bath has been covered in hardened lava stone.   □Photo: Peter French

The moon in the Puna sky illuminates the land of flame
and bloom.   □Photo: Nobu Nakayama

In the land of Pele, a *ti* leaf wrapped rock is offered as a *hookupu* or offering to the goddess of the volcano.
□Photo: Peter French

Facts About Hawaii: *The Big Island*

Hawaii County, encompassing the island of Hawaii, is the State of Hawaii's largest County in size. With an area of 4,034 square (land) miles, the "Big Island" is almost twice the combined size of all the other islands in the State. It measures 93 by 76 miles. It was formed by five volcanoes, two of which are still active, and is the youngest island in the Hawaiian chain. Ka Lae (South Point) is the southernmost point in the United States.

Principal industries in the County are sugarcane growing and milling, tourism, diversified agriculture and cattle ranching, and astronomy. Hawaii County also has the only coffee industry in the United States, the largest orchid growing business in the world, and an expanding export industry in macadamia nuts, papayas, and tropical flowers and foliage.

POPULATION

The estimated resident population of Hawaii County in 1992 was 130,500. Hilo is the County seat and the fourth largest city in the State. In addition to Hilo, the main population centers in the County are Kailua, Captain Cook, Honokaa, and Pahala.

In 1992, data on the ethnic makeup of the population of Hawaii County showed these percentages: Japanese, 19; Caucasian, 21; Filipino, 8, pure Hawaiians, 2; the other ethnic groups such as Chinese, Koreans, African-Americans, Samoans and Puerto Ricans are each about 1 or less. Hawaii County has no ethnic majority.

CLIMATE

There are wide variations in temperature and rainfall on the Big Island, due primarily to the range of elevation and location rather than to seasonal change.

Along the coastal regions, the climate is warm and semitropical. Average temperature in Hilo ranges from about 71° in February to about 76° in August.

In the higher areas, temperatures are lower. The average annual temperature at the 11,000-foot level of Mauna Loa is 44°. Frost occurs above the 4,000-foot level, and snow often covers the almost 14,000-foot peaks of Mauna Loa and Mauna Kea in the winter.

Rainfall varies markedly between the regions of the County, ranging from an annual rainfall of 300 inches at the 3,000-foot level northwest of Hilo to six inches near Kawaihae. The annual average has been 129 inches for the city of Hilo and 25 inches for Kailua.

TOURISM

In 1991, an estimated 1,188,630 westbound visitors visited the Big Island.

In 1991, Hawaii County had a total of 133 hotel and apartment-hotel units. Numerous new hotel units are planned in the County with many in ultra-luxury resorts on West Hawaii's Kona-Kohala Coast which is rapidly becoming one of the world's most lavish resort areas. New shopping centers, housing, and a variety of service establishments are being built, and infrastructure improvements sought, to meet the needs of residents and visitors.

AGRICULTURE

Agriculture is one of the major industries in Hawaii County. Although sugar acreage is expected to decline substantially, the island of Hawaii will remain the State's largest sugar producer. Three sugar companies in 1985 produced 2,686,000 tons of unprocessed cane.

Big Island cattle ranches, including Parker Ranch, one of the largest singly-owned ranches in the United States, produce over 65 percent of the volume of livestock marketed in the State.

Hawaii County raised approximately 64.0 million tons of the State's production of 81.0 million tons of fruit (other than pineapple). It supplies 37.1 of the 89.6 million tons of vegetables and melons grown in the State.

MANUFACTURING

In addition to the sugar mills in Hawaii County, there are many manufacturing plants. Lava rock; aggregate and concrete products; specialized heavy equipment; Hawaiian sportswear; pancake syrups; tropical fruit jams, purees, etc.; chocolate-macadamia nut candy; meats; and beverages are produced in the County.

SCIENTIFIC ACTIVITIES

The County of Hawaii offers unusual and unique natural advantages for scientific research in the fields of astronomy and geophysics. These include two mountain peaks rising more than 13,000 feet above sea level, clear uncontaminated air, mid-ocean location, relative closeness to the equator, still-active volcanoes and a wide variety of terrain and climatic conditions.

The 13,796-foot summit of Mauna Kea is recognized as the best ground-based site in the world for astronomical observations. Two 24-inch telescopes, an 88-inch optical/infrared telescope, and a NASA-funded 120-inch infrared are operated by the University of Hawaii. Other telescopes are Canada-France-Hawaii's 144-inch optical/infrared, and the United Kingdom's 150-inch infrared.

A Bibliography of Further Reading

For those who wish to probe deeper into the history, culture and beauty of Hawaii, the Big Island, the following works are recommended:

Bird, Isabella. *Six Months in the Sandwich Islands*. Rutland, Vermont: Charles Tuttle & Co., 1974.

Clark, John R. K. *Beaches of the Big Island*. Honolulu: University of Hawaii Press, 1985.

Daws, Gavan. *Shoal of Time*. Honolulu: University of Hawaii Press, 1968.

Day, A. Grove. *Mark Twain's Letters from Hawaii*. Honolulu: University of Hawaii Press, 1966.

Ellis, William. *Polynesian Researches: Hawaii*. Rutland, Vermont: Charles Tuttle & Co., 1976.

Emerson, Nathaniel B. *Pele and Hiiaka*. Honolulu Star-Bulletin, 1915.

Emerson, Nathaniel B. *The Unwritten Literature of Hawaii*. Rutland, Vermont: Charles Tuttle & Co., 1965.

Fornander, Abraham. *An Account of the Polynesian Race*. Rutland, Vermont: Charles Tuttle & Co., 1969.

Fuchs, Lawrence. *Hawaii Pono, A Social History*. N.Y.: Harcourt, Brace and World, Inc., 1961.

Haar, Francis. *Iolani Luahine*. Honolulu: Topgallant Publishing Company, 1985.

Handy, E.S.C., and Mary Kawena Pukui. *The Polynesian Family System in Ka'u, Hawaii*. Wellington, N.Z.: The Polynesian Society, 1958.

Kamakau, Samuel M. *The Ruling Chiefs of Hawaii*. Honolulu: Kamehameha Schools Press, 1961.

Krauss, Bob. *The Island Way*. Honolulu: Island Heritage, 1977.

Malo, David. *Hawaiian Antiquities*. Honolulu: Bishop Museum Special Publication No. 2, 1951.

Neal, Marie Catherine. *In Gardens of Hawaii*. Honolulu: Bishop Museum Press, 1965.

Pukui, Mary Kawena, and Samuel H. Elbert. *Hawaiian-English Dictionary*. Honolulu, University of Hawaii Press, 1986.

Ronck, Ronn. *Celebration: A Portrait of Hawaii Through the Songs of the Brothers Cazimero*. Honolulu, Mutual Publishing Co., 1984.

———. *Hawaii Almanac*. Honolulu: University of Hawaii Press, 1984.

Shook, E. Victoria. *Atlas of Hawaii*, 2nd ed. Honolulu, University of Hawaii Press, 1983.

Index

Graphic design by Rubin E. Young III
Composition by Ad Type, Inc.
Text set in 10/12 Caxton Book,
captions set in 9/10 Helvetica Bold,
Medium and Light.

Church, Hilo, Hawaii, T. H.

Volcano House, Hawaii.

Volcano House, Hawaii.